Trash TO TREASURE

*I*f you're in the habit of throwing away empty cans and boxes, worn-out sweaters, and plastic packaging, think again! Let us show you how to transform ordinary throwaways into glittering wonders! This Trash to Treasure *volume, devoted exclusively to Christmas, is packed with fun projects to fill your home with joy and cover your tree with splendor. It also has great gifts and presentation ideas to impress friends and family. In all, there are more than 120 projects that use "recycled" odds and ends. You'll have a happy Christmas that's easy on your pocketbook and friendly to the environment! We even offer "before" pictures to help you identify the "trash" in the projects. It's a snap to turn out perfect items time after time with our easy-to-follow instructions and full-color photographs. Start today to craft your way to your merriest holiday ever!*

Anne Childs

LEISURE ARTS, INC.
Little Rock, Arkansas

CHRISTMAS

EDITORIAL STAFF

Vice President and Editor-in-Chief: Anne Van Wagner Childs
Executive Director: Sandra Graham Case
Design Director: Patricia Wallenfang Sowers
Editorial Director: Susan Frantz Wiles
Publications Director: Kristine Anderson Mertes
Creative Art Director: Gloria Bearden

DESIGN
Designers: Diana Sanders Cates, Cherece Athy Cooper,
 Dani Martin, Sandra Spotts Ritchie, Billie Steward,
 Anne Pulliam Stocks, and Linda Diehl Tiano
Executive Assistant: Debra Smith
Design Assistant: Melanie Vaughan

TECHNICAL
Managing Editor: Barbara McClintock Vechik
Senior Technical Writer: Jennifer Potts Hutchings
Technical Writers: Susan McManus Johnson, Laura Lee Powell,
 Marley N. Washum, and Theresa Hicks Young
Copy Editor: Susan Frazier
Production Assistant: Sharon Gillam

EDITORIAL
Managing Editor: Linda L. Trimble
Associate Editor: Janice Teipen Wojcik
Assistant Editors: Terri Leming Davidson
 and Stacey Robertson Marshall

ART
Book/Magazine Graphics Art Director: Diane Thomas
Senior Graphics Illustrator: Linda Chambers
Graphics Illustrator: Michael A. Spigner
Color Technician: Mark Hawkins
Photography Stylists: Beth Carter, Ellen J. Clifton,
 Sondra Daniel, Karen Smart Hall, and Aurora Huston
Publishing Systems Administrator: Cindy Lumpkin
Publishing Systems Assistants: Myra Means

PROMOTIONS
Managing Editor: Alan Caudle
Associate Editor: Steven M. Cooper
Designer: Dale Rowett
Art Director: Linda Lovette Smart

BUSINESS STAFF

Publisher: Rick Barton
Vice President, Finance: Tom Siebenmorgen
Director of Corporate Planning and Development:
 Laticia Mull Cornett
Vice President, Retail Marketing: Bob Humphrey
Retail Marketing Director: Margaret Sweetin

Vice President, Sales: Ray Shelgosh
Vice President, National Accounts: Pam Stebbins
Vice President, Operations: Jim Dittrich
Comptroller, Operations: Rob Thieme
Retail Customer Service Manager: Wanda Price
Print Production Manager: Fred F. Pruss

Library of Congress Catalog Number 98-65089
Hardcover International Standard Book Number 1-57486-094-1
Softcover International Standard Book Number 1-57486-228-6

10 9 8 7 6 5 4 3

TABLE OF CONTENTS

all through the HOUSE 6

TABLE OF CONTENTS

trim the TREE 52

great GIFTS 82

TABLE OF CONTENTS

all WRAPPED up 108

all through the
HOUSE

*D*eck the halls with boughs of holly — and eye-catching decorations made from items you would ordinarily throw away! You'll have a ball choosing projects from our All Through the House collection, which is sprinkled with Santas, poinsettias, angels, and peppermint candies. Set the mood for a holly-jolly Christmas with cheerful snowmen crafted from fabric bolts, a twinkling tabletop tree made out of a tomato cage, and festive stockings crafted from neckties or flannel shirts. So plan now to fill your house — from mantel to dining room, kitchen to bath — with holiday magic. Simply turn the pages to select clever accent pieces you can make yourself from "recycled" materials!

STATELY NUTCRACKER

*Y*ou can create an impressive nutcracker — an endearing symbol of holiday fantasies — using the simplest of materials. Cardboard tubes from paper towel rolls shape this stately character's body, and his fancy belt buckle is a soda pop-top!

PAPER TUBE NUTCRACKER

Recycled items: two 5¼"h x ⅝" dia. cigar tubes with lids, paper towel tube, plastic lid, assorted gold trims, black ribbon, pull tab, and artificial fur

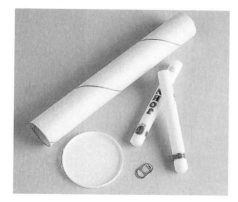

You will also need white, gold, flesh, pink, red, blue, and black acrylic paint; paintbrushes; tracing paper; transfer paper; hot glue gun; utility scissors; craft stick; clear acrylic spray sealer; and a teardrop-shaped acrylic jewel.

Refer to Painting Techniques, page 156, before beginning project. Allow paint and sealer to dry after each application.

1. Remove lids from cigar tubes. Cut 1" from top of each cigar tube.
2. Paint sections on cigar tubes for arms and on paper towel tube for body (Fig. 1).

Fig. 1

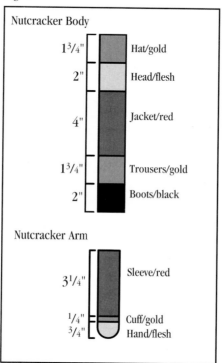

Nutcracker Body

1¾"	Hat/gold
2"	Head/flesh
4"	Jacket/red
1¾"	Trousers/gold
2"	Boots/black

Nutcracker Arm

3¼"	Sleeve/red
¼"	Cuff/gold
¾"	Hand/flesh

3. Trace face pattern, page 128, onto tracing paper. Use transfer paper to transfer face to head; paint face.
4. Paint 1½" inside top of body and cigar tube lids gold. Glue lids to tops of cigar tubes.
5. For nose, paint 1½" of one end of craft stick flesh. Trace nose pattern, page 128, onto tracing paper; cut out. Use pattern and utility scissors to cut nose from painted end of craft stick. Glue nose to face.
6. Trace feet pattern, page 128, onto tracing paper; cut out. Use pattern to cut feet from plastic lid. Paint feet black. Glue feet to body.
7. Apply one coat of sealer to body and arms.
8. Glue trims to body and arms as desired. Glue jewel to hat.
9. Glue one end of ribbon around center of pull tab. Wrap ribbon around container. Thread remaining ribbon end through pull tab; glue to secure. For beard, glue fur below mouth.
10. Glue arms to nutcracker.

VICTORIAN NOSEGAY

*P*aper roses add charm to this nostalgic nosegay, which is richly endowed with Victorian romance. Painted newspaper strips become handsome buds and blooms when folded, rolled, and glued. Finish the arrangement with a doily, silver spoon, and holiday embellishments.

NEWSPAPER NOSEGAY

Recycled items: newspaper, spoon, gold and plaid ribbons, and artificial greenery

You will also need red acrylic paint, paintbrush, hot glue gun, tracing paper, and a 6" dia. paper doily.

1. Cut three 3" x 13" pieces and one 13$^1/_2$" x 16$^1/_2$" piece from newspaper; paint red and allow to dry.
2. For each small rose, fold one end of a 3" x 13" piece $^1/_4$" to wrong side. Matching wrong sides and long edges, fold piece in half. With long folded edge at top and beginning with unfolded end, roll one-fourth of piece tightly to form rose center; glue to secure. Wrap remainder of piece loosely around center, folding small uneven pleats along bottom edge; glue bottom edge to secure.
3. For large rose, trace petal pattern,

page 128, onto tracing paper; cut out. Using pattern, cut six petals from remaining red paper piece. Curl side edges of each petal around a pencil (Fig. 1).

Fig. 1

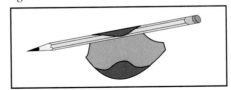

4. Glue petals around one small rose.
5. For nosegay, cut doily from outer edge to center. Overlapping cut edges $^1/_2$", shape doily into a cone; glue to secure. Trim $^1/_2$" from point of cone.
6. Insert handle of spoon through hole in cone; glue bowl of spoon in cone.
7. Tie gold ribbon into a bow. Arrange roses, bow, and greenery in cone; glue in place. Tie plaid ribbon into a bow around handle of spoon.

SEASON'S GREETINGS SHADE

A bright reminder of this merry season, our clever lampshade is a great way to display motifs from your favorite Christmas cards! Use cards you've received from special friends and relatives to create this lovely accent piece.

CHRISTMAS CARD LAMPSHADE

Recycled items: lampshade and Christmas cards

You will also need red and black spray paint, gold acrylic paint, paintbrush, natural sponge, decorative-edge craft scissors, craft glue, wood-tone spray, and clear acrylic spray sealer.

Refer to Painting Techniques, page 156, before beginning project. Allow paint, glue, wood-tone spray, and sealer to dry after each application.

1. Spray outside of shade red, inside of shade black, and paint top and bottom edges of shade gold. Sponge paint inside of shade gold.
2. Use craft scissors to cut desired motifs from cards; glue motifs to shade.
3. Lightly spray shade with wood-tone spray, then sealer.

BRANCHED-OUT "FAMILY TREE"

*A*s your family starts branching out, you can help everyone keep in touch with their roots with this clever snow-kissed "family tree." These fun-to-make remembrances are so economical and easy that you can make them for all your clan — from grandparents to siblings! The ornaments are crafted by mounting photocopies of snapshots to cardboard.

PHOTO TWIG TREE

Recycled items: cardboard, buttons, assorted fabrics, twigs, and rocks

You will also need black and white photocopies of family photographs, wood-tone spray, craft glue, tracing paper, black permanent fine-point marker, hot glue gun, jute twine, 18mm jingle bell, $1/8$"w red and green satin ribbon, pinking shears, $4^1/2$" dia. clay pot, 1"w green grosgrain ribbon, paintbrush, and artificial snowflakes.

Use hot glue for all gluing unless otherwise indicated. Allow wood-tone spray and glue to dry after each application unless otherwise indicated.

1. Trace heart pattern, page 129, onto tracing paper; cut out. For tree topper, draw around pattern on cardboard; cut out.
2. Use marker to write "Our Family" on tree topper. Beginning and ending at top center and trimming to fit, glue twine along edges of tree topper. Glue bell to top of tree topper, covering twine ends. Cut a 6" length each of red and green satin ribbon. Tie ribbons together into a bow; glue bow to top of tree topper.
3. Lightly spray photocopies with wood-tone spray. Use craft glue to glue photocopies to cardboard.
4. Centering image under pattern, draw around pattern on each photocopy; cut out. For each ornament, beginning and ending at top center and trimming to fit, glue twine along edge of heart. Glue button at top of ornament, covering twine ends. For hanger, cut a 3" length of twine; glue ends to back of ornament. Cut a 6" length of red or green satin ribbon. Tie ribbon into a bow. Glue bow to hanger.
5. Use pinking shears to cut $1^1/2$" squares from fabric. Overlapping edges as necessary to cover pot, use craft glue to glue fabric to pot. Overlapping ends at

back, glue a 15" length of grosgrain ribbon around rim of pot. Tie 16" lengths of red and green satin ribbons together into a bow; glue to rim.
6. Cut 5", 7", 9", 11", and 13" lengths from twigs for branches and a 19" length from one twig for trunk. Referring to Fig. 1 for branch placement and wrapping in a crisscross direction, use twine to tie branches to trunk; glue ends to secure. Position trunk in center of pot; fill pot with rocks.

Fig. 1

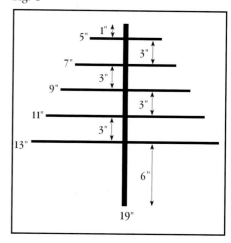

7. Glue tree topper to top of tree. Hang ornaments on tree as desired. Using paintbrush, apply craft glue to areas where snowflakes are desired. While glue is still wet, apply snowflakes to tree.

For a colorful country touch, add whimsical reminders of our fine-feathered friends to your holiday decor. Creatively crafted from paper cartons, these fanciful birdhouses are topped with roofs made of cardboard, an egg carton, and pieces of flattened cans.

Refer to Painting Techniques, page 156, before beginning project. Allow primer, paint, and glue to dry after each application. Use hot glue for all gluing unless otherwise indicated. Use garden clippers to cut twigs.

YELLOW BIRDHOUSE

Recycled items: paper carton at least 3"w x 9"h, cardboard, twigs, and a pinecone

You will also need white spray primer; yellow, gold, red, green, and black acrylic paint; paintbrushes; hot glue gun; tracing paper; transfer paper; craft knife; cutting mat; black permanent fine-point marker; foam brush; craft glue; sheet moss; garden clippers; push pin; and wood-tone spray.

1. Open top of carton. Spray carton with three coats of primer. Paint inside of carton black. Use hot glue to reseal carton.

2. Paint roof red and birdhouse yellow.

3. Trace Border A and Design A, page 130, onto tracing paper. Use transfer paper to transfer border around bottom of birdhouse and design to front of birdhouse. Use craft knife to carefully cut openings in birdhouse. Paint border and design. Use marker to draw "stitches" around holes and to outline design as desired.

4. For roof panels, refer to Fig. 1 to measure width and height of roof; add ³/₄" to height. Cut two pieces of cardboard the determined measurements.

Fig. 1

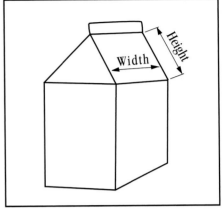

5. Use foam brush to apply craft glue to one side of each panel. Press sheet moss into glue, covering panels. Trim sheet moss to fit panels. Glue roof panels to birdhouse.

6. Trimming to fit, glue twigs along edges of roof and along bottom of birdhouse.

7. Break one section from pinecone. Use gold acrylic paint to add highlights to pinecone section; glue to peak of roof.

8. For each perch, use push pin to make a pilot hole ¹/₄" below each opening. Cut a 1¹/₂" long twig; insert in hole.

9. Lightly spray birdhouse with wood-tone spray.

RED BIRDHOUSE

Recycled items: paper carton at least 2³/₄"w x 4³/₄"h, corrugated cardboard, and twigs

You will also need white spray primer; yellow, red, green, and black acrylic paint; paintbrushes; hot glue gun; tracing paper;

Continued on page 16

transfer paper; craft knife; cutting mat; star-shaped wooden cutout; black permanent fine-point marker; garden clippers; push pin; and wood-tone spray.

1. Follow Step 1 of Yellow Birdhouse, page 15, to prepare carton.
2. Paint roof green and birdhouse red.
3. Trace Border B and Design B, page 130, onto tracing paper. Use transfer paper to transfer border and design to front of birdhouse. Use craft knife to carefully cut opening in birdhouse. Paint border and design. Paint wooden cutout yellow. Use marker to outline design as desired and to draw "stitches" along edges of wooden cutout.
4. Follow Step 4 of Yellow Birdhouse to make roof panels; glue panels to birdhouse.
5. Trimming to fit, glue twigs along edges on front of roof and along bottom of birdhouse. Glue wooden cutout to peak of roof.
6. For perch, use push pin to make a pilot hole $1/4$" below opening. Cut a $1^1/2$" long twig; insert in hole.
7. Lightly spray birdhouse with wood-tone spray.

GREEN BIRDHOUSE

Recycled items: paper carton at least $3^3/8$"w x $6^1/2$"h, papier-mâché egg carton, twigs, and an aluminum beverage can
You will also need white spray primer; yellow, red, green, and black acrylic paint; paintbrushes; hot glue gun; tracing paper; transfer paper; craft knife; cutting mat; liner brush; black permanent fine-point marker; garden clippers; push pin; and wood-tone spray.

1. Follow Step 1 of Yellow Birdhouse, page 15, to prepare carton.
2. Paint carton green.
3. Trace Border C and Design C, page 131, onto tracing paper. Use transfer paper to transfer border around top of birdhouse and design to one side of birdhouse. Use craft knife to carefully cut opening in birdhouse. Paint border and design. Use liner brush to add "X's" and dots as desired. Use marker to outline border and draw "stitches" along edges of designs.
4. Follow Step 4 of Yellow Birdhouse to make roof panels from egg carton; glue panels to birdhouse.
5. Trimming to fit, glue twigs along edges on front of roof and along bottom of birdhouse.
6. Cut through opening and down to bottom of beverage can; cut away top and bottom from can. Flatten can piece. Trace moon from Design C onto tracing paper; cut out. Use marker to draw around pattern on can piece; cut out. Glue moon to peak of roof.
7. For perch, use push pin to make a pilot hole $1/4$" below opening. Cut a $1^1/2$" long twig; insert in hole.
8. Lightly spray birdhouse with wood-tone spray.

TOPIARY BIRDHOUSE

Recycled items: paper carton at least $2^1/4$"w x 4"h, $4^1/2$-oz. can, aluminum beverage can, twigs, button, and 6" long by $1/4$" dia. stick for trunk
You will also need white spray primer; yellow, red, green, and black acrylic paint; paintbrushes; hot glue gun; red spray paint; tracing paper; transfer paper; craft knife; cutting mat; black permanent fine-point marker; garden clippers; push pin; floral foam; foam brush; craft glue; sheet moss; and wood-tone spray.

1. Follow Step 1 of Yellow Birdhouse, page 15, to prepare carton.
2. Paint roof green and birdhouse black. For topiary base, spray paint $4^1/2$-oz. can red.
3. Trace Design D, page 130, onto tracing paper. Use transfer paper to transfer design to one side of birdhouse. Use craft knife to carefully cut opening in birdhouse. Paint design on birdhouse. Use marker to outline outer edges of design and to draw "stitches" along edges of heart.
4. Cut through opening and down to bottom of beverage can; cut away top and bottom from can. Flatten can piece.
5. Follow Step 4 of Yellow Birdhouse to make roof panels from can piece; glue panels to birdhouse.
6. Trimming to fit, glue twigs along edges on front of roof and along bottom of birdhouse. Glue button to peak of roof.
7. For perch, use push pin to make a pilot hole $1/4$" below opening. Cut a $1^1/2$" long twig; insert in hole.
8. Fill base with floral foam. Use foam brush to apply craft glue to floral foam. Cover top of base with moss.
9. Cut an "X" in center of bottom of birdhouse slightly smaller than diameter of trunk. Insert one end of trunk into floral foam and opposite end through hole in bottom of birdhouse.
10. Lightly spray topiary with wood-tone spray.

"WRAPPED" WITH CHEER

Welcome your friends and family with a perky door wreath fashioned from wrapping paper and brown paper bags! Trimmed using decorative-edge scissors, paper squares are shaped into scrunchy bundles and glued to a foam wreath. The circle is then accented with baubles and a beautiful bow.

GIFT WRAP WREATH

Recycled items: wrapping paper and brown paper bags

You will also need decorative-edge craft scissors, pencil, craft glue, 16" dia. foam wreath, bead garland, hot glue gun, glass ornaments, and $2^{1}/_{2}$"w wired ribbon.

Use hot glue for all gluing unless otherwise indicated.

1. Using craft scissors, cut 4" squares from wrapping paper and paper bags.
2. Place eraser end of pencil at center of right side of one square. Loosely twist square around pencil (Fig. 1). Dip paper-covered end of pencil in craft glue; position on wreath and remove pencil. Repeat until wreath is covered. Allow to dry.

Fig. 1

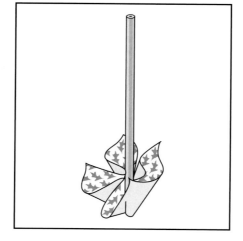

3. Wrap garland around wreath; glue ends to secure. Glue ornaments to wreath as desired.
4. For bow, cut two 22" lengths and one 18" length from ribbon. Overlapping $^{1}/_{2}$", glue short ends of each 22" length together to form two loops. With overlaps at center back, tie remaining ribbon around centers of loops. Arrange and glue bow on wreath.

PEPPERMINT NOEL

*S*pelling out a cordial "Noel," this peppermint-striped garland will delight candy cane lovers. The spirited decoration is made from paper tubes, with colorful ribbons forming the stripes.

PAPER TUBE "NOEL" GARLAND

Recycled items: seven paper towel tubes, six toilet paper tubes, and cardboard

You will also need white fabric; spray adhesive; hot glue gun; red, red-and-white striped, and narrow green polka-dot ribbons; plastic wrap; and artificial greenery garland.

1. Cut seven $5^1/2$" x $12^1/2$" and six $5^1/2$" x 6" pieces from white fabric.
2. Apply spray adhesive to wrong side of fabric pieces. Leaving $3/4$" at top and bottom of tube, wrap each paper towel tube with one $5^1/2$" x $12^1/2$" fabric piece and each toilet paper tube with one $5^1/2$" x 6" fabric piece. Glue fabric ends to inside of tubes.
3. For peppermint stripes, glue red and red-and-white striped ribbon lengths around tubes as desired.
4. With ends of wrap extending $1^1/2$" at each end, wrap each tube with plastic wrap. Form letters by tying connecting ends together with polka dot ribbon (Fig. 1). Tie ribbon around each remaining end.

Fig. 1

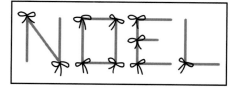

5. To reinforce letters, cut ten $1/2$" x $2^1/2$" strips of cardboard; glue across back of letters at each angle. Glue letters to garland.
6. Cut six 26" lengths of red ribbon. Tie two ribbon lengths together into a bow. Repeat to make a total of three bows. Glue bows to garland.

SWEATER STOCKING

*H*ow creative! It's easy to "recycle" a once-favored sweater into a handsome Christmas stocking! A few snips and some quick sewing give your outgrown or outdated garment a second life as an eye-catching Yuletide accent.

SWEATER STOCKING

Recycled item: sweater

You will also need tracing paper, fabric marking pen, and ⁷/₈" dia. covered button kit (optional).

1. Matching grey lines and arrows, trace stocking top and stocking bottom patterns, pages 142 and 143, onto tracing paper; cut out.
2. Turn sweater wrong side out. Aligning top edge of stocking pattern with bottom edge of sweater, follow *Sewing Shapes*, page 159, to make stocking.
3. For hanger, cut a ³/₄" x 6¹/₂" piece from remaining sweater scrap. Matching right sides and long edges, fold piece in half; sew along long edge. Turn right side out. Matching short, raw edges with heel seam of stocking, sew hanger to stocking.
4. If desired, follow manufacturer's instructions to cover buttons with sweater scraps. Sew buttons to stocking.

HOMESPUN HOLY FAMILY

*T*his easy-to-craft Nativity set adds a reverent touch to your country Christmas decor! Using cotton batting, homespun fabrics, and curly doll hair, you can transform foam balls and juice bottles into charming Holy Family figures.

JUICE BOTTLE NATIVITY

Recycled items: two small juice bottles and rubber bands

You will also need a hot glue gun, two 2" dia. plastic foam balls, muslin, fabric, two chenille stems, wire cutters, four 15mm wooden beads, batting, string, curly doll hair, cosmetic blush, black permanent fine-point marker, jute twine, fiberfill, and a small basket.

MARY

1. For head, remove lid from bottle; glue ball to top of bottle. Wrap a 6" square of muslin around head; gather at neck. Use rubber band to secure.
2. For robe, cut a 7" x 19" piece from fabric. Press one long edge $1/2$" to wrong side; glue to secure. Overlapping $1/2$", glue short edges together to form a tube. With raw edge at neck, place tube over bottle. Gather fabric at neck under rubber band.
3. For arms, cut a 9" length from chenille stem; glue one bead to each end of stem. Wrap stem with batting. Cut a 4" x 9" piece from fabric. Overlapping long edges, loosely wrap fabric around arms; glue to secure. Knot string around each wrist; trim ends. Wrap arms around body; glue at center back.
4. Glue hair on head. For face, apply blush for cheeks and use marker to make dots for eyes.
5. For scarf, fringe each short end of a 4" x 17" strip of fabric. Wrap scarf around head and secure at waist with twine.

JOSEPH

1. Using a 7" x 15" piece of fabric for robe, follow Steps 1 - 3 of Mary to make body. For scarf, fringe each short end of a 4" x 17" strip of fabric. Wrap scarf around shoulders and secure at waist with twine.
2. Glue hair to head. For beard, glue hair to chin. Use marker to make dots for eyes.
3. For hood, cover head with a 4" x $8 1/2$" piece of fabric, secure with twine.

BABY JESUS

1. Gather a 5" square of muslin around a $1 1/2$" dia. ball of fiberfill; use rubber band to secure. Glue hair to Baby. Use marker to make dots for eyes.
2. Glue Baby to one corner of a 10" square of batting. Fold side edges around face; spot glue at chin to secure.
3. Place Baby in basket; arrange batting as desired for blanket.

WOODLAND GARLAND

*M*other Nature's own festive finery adds a woodsy feel to this holiday trim. Highlighted with mossy stars, a garland of gilded pinecones and sweet gum balls is accented with scraps of ribbon tied into bows.

NATURALS GARLAND

Recycled items: pinecones, sweet gum pods, cardboard, embroidery floss, and ribbon

You will also need gold acrylic paint, paintbrush, gold spray paint, star anise, tracing paper, foam brush, craft glue, sheet moss, sharp needle, and a hot glue gun.

Use craft glue for all gluing unless otherwise indicated. Allow paint and glue to dry after each application.

1. Use acrylic paint to highlight pinecones. Spray paint sweet gum pods and star anise.
2. Trace pattern, page 132, onto tracing paper; cut out. Draw around pattern on cardboard desired number of times; cut out stars.
3. Use foam brush to apply glue to each star; press moss into glue. Trim moss even with edges of star. Glue star anise to center of star.
4. Use needle to thread sweet gum pods onto floss.
5. Tie ribbon into bows. Arrange and hot glue pinecones and stars to floss between pods; glue bows to pinecones. Knot ends to secure.

YULETIDE CANDLES

*N*o one would guess that this attractive Yuletide arrangement is actually a collection of holiday odds and ends. To assemble the centerpiece, accent pillar candles with pretty ribbons and cutouts from Christmas cards you've saved. Surround the candles with greenery, bead garland, and glass ornaments.

EMBELLISHED CANDLE CENTERPIECE

Recycled items: Christmas cards, satin ribbon, artificial greenery, bead garland, glass ball ornaments, and a silk flower

You will also need craft glue, wired ribbon, pillar candles, and a glass plate.

1. Cut desired motifs from cards.
2. Glue ribbons and motifs to candles as desired.
3. Tie a length of wired ribbon into a bow. Arrange candles, bow, greenery, garland, ornaments, and flower on plate.

HEAVENLY HOLIDAY ANGEL

Give your holiday decor a heavenly touch with our adorable Christmas angel! Beneath the festive gown and curly hair of this bow-winged heavenly spirit, you'll find a beverage bottle body and a head made from a light bulb!

LIGHT BULB AND BOTTLE ANGEL

Recycled items: light bulb, medium-size bottle with opening large enough to accommodate base of light bulb, gold trim, rubber band, and an artificial poinsettia

You will also need peach, pink, red, and black acrylic paint; paintbrushes; hot glue gun; fabric; curly doll hair; gold craft wire; 2"w gold mesh wired ribbon; and narrow gold wired ribbon.

Allow paint to dry after each application. Match right sides and raw edges and use a $1/4$" seam allowance for all sewing unless otherwise indicated.

1. For head, paint light bulb peach. Paint face on light bulb. Glue base of bulb into opening of bottle.
2. For dress, measure height of bottle; add 2". Cut two pieces from fabric 12" (top and bottom) by the determined measurement (sides). Press top and bottom edges 1" to wrong side. Stitch in place. Leaving a 2" opening in each side for arms, sew sides of dress together (Fig. 1).

Fig. 1

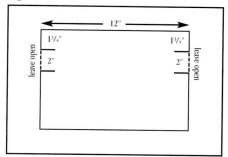

3. For arms, cut a 4" x 14" piece from fabric. Sew long edges together, forming a tube. Turn tube right side out. Tie a knot at center of tube. Glue ends of arms into openings in sides of dress.
4. For hem, glue trim along one edge of dress. Place dress over bottle with hem even with bottom of bottle. Gather dress around neck of angel; secure with rubber band. Glue trim around gathers, covering rubber band.
5. Glue doll hair to head. For halo, cut an 11" length of wire. Form a 2" dia. circle at one end of wire; glue opposite end to back of head.
6. For wings, cut three 18" lengths and one 5" length from gold mesh ribbon. Overlapping ends 1", glue short ends of each 18" length together to form three separate loops. With overlaps at center back, pinch loops together at center. Wrap 5" length around pinched center; glue to secure. Glue wings to back of dress.
7. Cut two 20" lengths of narrow gold ribbon. Tie ribbons together into a bow with 4" loops and 5" streamers. Glue bow to knot in arms. Glue poinsettia to center of bow.

FOLKSY FLANNEL STOCKING

Santa and his elves will surely take a fancy to our cozy flannel stocking! Featuring a patchwork cuff and welting made from old flannel shirts, this imaginative stocking is a heartwarming addition to your down-home Christmas decor.

FLANNEL SHIRT STOCKING

Recycled items: flannel shirts and seven buttons

You will also need two 9½" x 15" pieces of fabric for stocking, two 9½" x 15" pieces of fabric for lining, tracing paper, 42" length of ¼" dia. cord for welting, two 2" x 22" strips of fabric for fringe, and embroidery floss.

Match right sides and raw edges and use a ¼" seam allowance for all sewing unless otherwise indicated.

1. Wash, dry, and press all fabrics.
2. Aligning grey lines and arrows, trace stocking top and stocking bottom patterns, pages 142 and 143, onto tracing paper. Draw a second line ¼" outside traced line along sides and bottom of pattern. Cut out pattern along top and outer lines.
3. Place stocking fabric pieces together. Cutting through both layers of fabric, use pattern to cut out stocking front and back. Repeat for lining pieces.
4. For welting, cut a 2" x 42" bias strip from shirts (pieced as necessary). Press one end ½" to wrong side. Beginning ½" from folded edge, center cord on wrong side of strip; fold strip over cord. Beginning ½" from folded end, use a zipper foot to baste close to cord along length of strip. Trim seam allowance to ¼".
5. Beginning with unpressed end, matching raw edges, and placing welting on right side of front of stocking, baste welting along side and bottom edges of stocking front. At each end of welting, open bias strip and trim ½" of cord; rebaste welting. Place stocking front and back together. Using a zipper foot, leaving top edge open, and sewing as close to welting as possible, sew stocking pieces together. Clip curves and turn right side out; press.

6. Leaving top edge open, sew lining pieces together; do not turn. Matching seams and raw edges, place lining inside stocking. Baste raw edges together.
7. For cuff, cut fourteen 2½" squares from shirts. Sew seven squares together end to end to make one row; repeat to make a total of two rows. Matching long edges, sew rows together.
8. For fringe, matching wrong side to right side, baste fabric strips together along one long edge. Clip strips at ½" intervals along opposite edge to ½" from basting thread. Pull basting thread, gathering fringe to fit long edge of cuff. Sew fringe to cuff. Press seam allowance to wrong side of cuff. Matching right sides and short ends, fold cuff in half. Sew short ends together to form a tube; turn right side out.
9. Matching right side of cuff to wrong side of stocking and seamline of cuff to heel side seamline of stocking, place cuff inside stocking. Sew cuff and stocking together. Fold cuff down over stocking.
10. For hanger, cut an 8½" strip from buttonhole placket of one shirt. Matching wrong sides, sew short ends of strip together. Sew a button to heel side seamline at top of stocking. Aligning two buttonholes, button hanger to stocking.
11. Tying floss at front, sew buttons to cuff as desired.

ADORABLE ANGEL

*S*urprise! Our adorable
Christmas angel is shaped around
a beverage bottle! Gold paint
transforms a mesh produce bag
and plastic lid into shining wings
and a halo. The little angel's crew
sock head is crowned with "hair"
made from dried baby's breath.

SOCK-COVERED BOTTLE ANGEL

Recycled items: adult-size white crew
sock, 10-oz. beverage bottle with lid,
3" dia. plastic lid, straight pin, mesh
produce bag, and gold cord

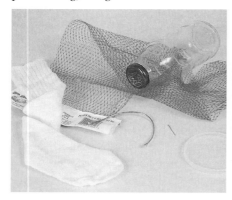

You will also need a 2" dia. plastic foam
ball, thread, tracing paper, white felt, craft
glue, gold dimensional paint,
4" dia. white doily, craft stick, white
acrylic paint, paintbrush, dried baby's
breath, brown permanent fine-point
marker, gold spray paint, and a miniature
wreath.

*Allow glue and paint to dry after each
application.*

1. Place foam ball in toe of sock; gather
sock around ball. Knot a length of thread
around gathers. Pull sock over bottle.

Roll remainder of sock into a 1 1/2" cuff at
bottom of bottle.

2. Trace sleeve pattern, page 129, onto
tracing paper. Using pattern, cut two
sleeves from white felt. Glue each sleeve
closed along long cut edges. Glue small
end of each sleeve to back of angel.

3. Use dimensional paint to outline top
edge of cuff at bottom of bottle, open
edges of each sleeve, and design on doily.

4. For arms, cut 2" from each end of craft
stick; paint white. With rounded ends
extending 1/2", glue arms in sleeves.

5. Cut doily from outer edge to center. Cut
a 1" dia. circle from center of doily. Place
doily around angel's neck; glue edges
together.

6. Glue baby's breath to head for hair. Use
marker to draw eyes on face.

7. For halo, use dimensional paint to
paint inside rim of plastic lid and add
accents to outside of rim. Use straight pin
to attach halo to head.

8. For wings, cut a 10" square from mesh
bag; spray paint piece gold. Gather piece
at center; secure with thread. Glue wings
to back of angel. Cover thread with
dimensional paint.

9. Tie gold cord into a bow to fit on
wreath. Glue bow to wreath. Glue arms to
wreath.

CANDLELIGHT AND HOLLY

*E*ncircling a trio of pristine pillar candles, our handsome grapevine wreath is bedecked with holly. The bright crimson "berries" are made by painting metal twist-off bottle caps, and the "leaves" are crafted from flattened and painted pieces of beverage cans.

CANS AND CAPS WREATH CENTERPIECE

Recycled items: seven aluminum beverage cans and bottle caps

You will also need tracing paper; black permanent fine-point marker; white spray primer; white, red, green, and black acrylic paint; paintbrushes; 12" dia. grapevine wreath; hot glue gun; 32" length of 2"w wired ribbon; and three various size candles.

Allow primer and paint to dry after each application.

1. Cut through opening and down to bottom of each beverage can; cut top and bottom from each can. Flatten can pieces.
2. Trace pattern, page 129, onto tracing paper; cut out. Use marker to draw

around pattern twice on each can piece. Cut leaves from can pieces.
3. Apply two coats of primer to leaves and bottle caps.
4. Paint both sides of each leaf green. Paint black veins on leaves.

5. For berries, paint bottle caps red. Paint white highlights on each berry.
6. Arrange and glue leaves and berries on wreath. Tie ribbon into a bow; glue to wreath. Place candles in center of wreath.

TINY TREASURES

*C*overed with a festive sprinkling of "recycled" odds and ends, this tiny tree is a Yuletide treasure! Featuring ornaments assembled from bottle caps, buttons, and foam, the tree has a gilded garland crafted from drinking straws. A doily tree skirt completes the look.

TINY TREASURES TREE

Recycled items: wired ribbon, plastic twist-off bottle caps, drinking straws, pull tabs, gold ribbon and trim, foam food trays, and buttons

You will also need 11" dia. doily, 18" artificial tree with removable stand, hot glue gun, gold and red spray paint, thread, tracing paper, craft knife, cutting mat, foam brush, craft glue, gold glitter, wire cutters, white cloth-covered craft wire, and assorted gold beads.

Allow paint to dry after each application. Use hot glue for all gluing unless otherwise indicated.

1. For tree skirt, fold doily in half from left to right and again from top to bottom. Cut away ¹/₂" of folded point. Unfold tree skirt. Insert trunk of tree through opening in skirt and into tree stand. Tie two 18" lengths of wired ribbon into bows. Glue bows to tree skirt and tree top.

2. Bend pull tabs 90° at center. Paint straws and pull tabs gold and bottle caps red.

3. For garland, cut straws into ¹/₂" lengths. String pieces onto thread. Tie thread ends together to secure. Arrange garland on tree.

4. For each round ornament, glue one end of pull tab in bottle cap. Tie an 8" length of ribbon into a bow; glue to top of pull tab. Glue trim across top and down each side of ornament.

5. Trace star pattern, page 129, onto tracing paper; cut out. Draw around pattern desired number of times on foam tray. Use craft knife to cut out stars. Use foam brush to apply craft glue to one side of each star. While glue is still wet, generously sprinkle glitter over glue. Shake gently to remove excess glitter.

6. For each button ornament, thread one bead onto a 4" length of wire; twist wires together to secure. Working through two holes on buttons, thread buttons and beads onto wire. Form wire end into a hanger.

7. Hang round and button ornaments on tree. Glue stars to tree as desired.

Add a touch of Christmas to your bath with festive glycerin soaps nestled in a handsome holiday basket. Shaped in plastic muffin containers, the soaps are accented with seasonal stickers.

DECORATED SOAPS

Recycled items: a plastic muffin container, can for melting soap, and newspaper

You will also need nonstick cooking spray, pre-scored glycerin soap blocks, seasonal stickers, and foam brush.

1. Spray inside of muffin container with cooking spray.
2. Substituting pre-scored glycerin soap blocks for wax, follow *Melting Wax*, page 157, and Step 2 of *Setting Wicks*, page 158, to melt and pour soap into muffin container.
3. Allow soaps to harden. Remove soaps from muffin container.
4. Center and apply stickers to soaps. Use foam brush to apply melted soap over stickers; allow to harden.

A perfectly packaged collection of naturally wonderful delights, our ingenious tree began as a tomato cage! To make this tabletop tree, a gilded cage is lined with bubble wrap, then accented with twinkling lights, a gilded pinecone and leaves, and spray-painted foam-tray stars.

TOMATO CAGE TREE

Recycled items: tomato cage, large bubble wrap, foam food trays, magnolia leaves, pinecone, and wired ribbon

You will also need grey spray primer, gold and silver Design Master® spray paint, fine-gauge craft wire, wire cutters, string of mini lights, gold bead garland, hot glue gun, small and large star-shaped cookie cutters, craft knife, cutting mat, foam brush, white latex paint, silver dimensional paint, nail, and gold metallic thread.

Allow primer and paint to dry after each application.

1. Spray cage with primer, then gold paint.
2. Wire post ends of cage together (top).
3. Beginning by wiring first light on plug end to bottom ring, wire lights on cage vertically between posts and around bottom ring. Wrap socket end around top of cage and allow lights to hang in center. Wire garland to cage along lights and rings.
4. Line inside of cage with bubble wrap; glue to secure.
5. For desired number of stars, press cookie cutters into foam tray. Use craft knife to cut out stars.
6. Use foam brush to paint stars white. Spray paint stars, magnolia leaves, and pinecone gold. Lightly spray leaves and several stars silver. Use dimensional paint to add dots and wavy stripes on stars.
7. Use a nail to punch a hole in top of each star.
8. Arrange and glue leaves on tree. Use 6" lengths of metallic thread to tie stars to tree.
9. Wire a cluster of stars around top of tree. Glue pinecone to top of tree.
10. Tie ribbon into a bow around base of pinecone.

"UN-CAN-NY" SNOWMAN CHIMES

A dd a wintry chime to your holiday festivities with our cheerful tin can snowman. Craft this whimsical music maker by painting and assembling "recycled" cans and lids.

Recycled items: aluminum beverage can, 5" dia. plastic lid for hat brim, 8-oz. pineapple can for hat, 46-oz. juice can for head, four assorted tops from cans, plastic handle from detergent box for hatband, and artificial greenery

You will also need wire cutters; medium-gauge craft wire; pencil; orange and red acrylic paint; paintbrushes; white spray primer; white, blue, and black spray paint; white paint pen; hammer; nail; hot glue gun; and clear nylon thread.

Allow paint and primer to dry after each application.

1. For nose, wrap a 6" length of wire around the pointed end of a pencil to form nose. Paint nose orange.
2. Cut through opening and down to bottom of beverage can; cut away top and bottom of can. Flatten can piece.
3. Spray can piece, all cans, can tops, plastic lid, and handle with primer. Paint can piece, hat, and lid black, head white, can tops blue, and hatband red. Use paint pen to draw snowflakes and borders onto both sides of can tops.
4. Rough cut two shapes for eyes and five shapes for mouth from can piece. Use hammer and nail to punch two holes 1/4" apart in each eye and one hole in center of each mouth shape.
5. With closed end of head at top, punch two holes 1/4" apart for each eye, one hole for nose, and two holes 2 1/4" apart for ends of mouth.
6. Insert wide end of nose through hole for nose; twist wire inside head to secure. Use wire to attach eyes to head. For mouth, cut an 8" length of wire. Thread mouth shapes onto wire. Insert wire ends into holes for mouth; twist ends of wire together inside head to secure. Arrange mouth shapes; glue in place.
7. Punch two holes 1/4" apart at centers of hat brim and closed ends of hat and head. For hanger, form a 1" loop at center of a 14" length of wire. Insert wire ends through holes in hat, hat brim, then head; twist ends together to secure.
8. Glue hat to hat brim and hat brim to head. Glue hatband around base of hat, trimming ends as necessary. Glue greenery to hat.
9. For chimes, punch a hole close to edge in each can top. Punch four evenly spaced holes along bottom edge of head. Use clear thread to attach chimes to head.

COUNTRY CASUAL WREATH

Our pretty poinsettia wreath lets you share woodsy greetings with all your holiday visitors! This Yuletide welcomer features poinsettias fashioned from grocery bags, along with naturals from your yard, including acorns, sweet gum pods, and pinecones.

PAPER BAG POINSETTIA WREATH

Recycled items: brown paper bags, poster board, scraps of ribbon, and assorted naturals (we used pinecones, sweet gum pods, acorns, and assorted nuts)

You will also need yellow, light red, red, dark red, green, and dark green acrylic paint; natural sponges; tracing paper; red and green permanent fine-point markers; drawing compass; craft glue; matte acrylic spray sealer; 18" dia. grapevine wreath; and a hot glue gun.

Allow paint, glue, and sealer to dry after each application. Use craft glue for all gluing unless otherwise indicated.

1. For each poinsettia, cut bag open along one fold and cut away bottom; press with warm, dry iron.
2. From bag, cut a 14" x 16" piece for petals, a 7" x 9" piece for leaves, and a 7" square piece for flower centers.
3. Follow *Sponge Painting*, page 157, to paint paper for petals light red, then red; paper for leaves green, then dark green; and both sides of paper for flower centers yellow.
4. Trace patterns, page 133, onto tracing paper; cut out. Using patterns, cut seven large and five small petals from red paper and two leaves from green paper.
5. Working from wide end to narrow end, use a dry sponge piece to streak petals with dark red paint and leaves with dark green paint. Use red marker to draw veins on petals and green marker to draw veins on leaves. Crumple petals and leaves lightly, then smooth out.
6. Use compass to draw a 1¹/₂" dia. circle on poster board; cut out. Beginning with large petals and overlapping edges as necessary, arrange and glue large petals, then small petals around poster board circle.
7. For flower centers, tear nine ³/₄" dia. pieces from yellow paper; roll into small balls. Glue balls at center of petals. Arrange and glue leaves around back of poster board circle.
8. Lightly spray each poinsettia with one coat of spray sealer.
9. Arrange flowers on wreath; hot glue to secure. Tie ribbon into a bow. Arrange bow and naturals on wreath; hot glue to secure.

FOLKSY APPLIQUÉD STOCKINGS

*K*ick off a down-home
country Christmas with festive
appliquéd stockings. It's easy to
craft the charming accents using
fabric scraps, fusible web, and
instant coffee for the dye!

CREW SOCK STOCKINGS

Recycled items: adult-size white crew
socks, fabrics, and buttons

You will also need instant coffee, paper-
backed fusible web, decorative-edge craft
scissors, batting, black permanent fine-
point marker, black embroidery floss, and
jute twine.

1. For stockings, follow *Coffee Dyeing,*
page 156, to dye each sock.
2. For cuff, measure around top of sock;
add ¹/₂". Cut a strip of fabric 8"w by the
determined measurement. Matching long
edges and wrong sides, press strip in half.
Place cuff inside sock with short ends
overlapping at back. Matching raw edge
of cuff to sock opening, sew in place. Fold
cuff down over top of stocking.
3. For appliqués, trace desired patterns,
page 134, and heel and toe areas of
stocking onto paper side of web. Using
craft scissors to cut out appliqués, follow

Steps 2 - 5 of *Making Appliqués,*
page 157, to make and fuse appliqués to
stocking.
4. Fuse one 3" square of fabric to each
side of a 3" square of batting. Trace
desired pattern, page 134, onto tracing
paper. Using pattern, cut shape from fused
square. Use marker to draw "stitches"
along edges of shape.

5. Using floss and one button, sew shape
to cuff. Attach additional buttons to
stocking as desired.
6. Cut a 16" length of twine. Leaving 3" at
each end, knot ends together. Use floss to
attach knot to cuff.

CANDYLAND COTTAGES

*S*ugar and spice and
everything nice goes into
ordinary gingerbread houses.
But our fun-to-make cottages
have surprising "ingredients" —
foam peanut roofs, bottle cap
"peppermint" windows, gum
wrapper doors, and walls
covered with paper bags!

CARTON COTTAGES

Recycled items: one-pint cartons, brown
paper bag, sand, 5" square pieces of
cardboard, twist-off bottle caps, gum
wrappers, straw candy wrappers, and
foam peanuts

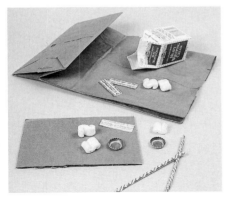

You will also need spray adhesive, hot
glue gun, white spray paint, white spray
primer, red acrylic paint, paintbrush,
tracing paper, white dimensional paint,
stencil brush, and textured snow paint.

*Allow paint and primer to dry after
each application.*

1. For each cottage, fully open top of
carton. Measure distance around carton.
Measure height of opened carton. Cut a
piece from paper bag the determined
measurements. Apply spray adhesive to
wrong side of paper bag. Beginning at

one back corner, smooth bag around
carton. Fill carton with sand; hot glue to
reseal.

2. Spray paint cardboard piece white.
Glue paper-covered carton to center of
one cardboard piece.

3. For peppermint, spray bottle cap with
primer. Use red paint to freehand candy
design on cap.

4. Cutting all pieces from gum wrappers,
cut a 1" x 2½" door, two 1⅛" square

windows, and a ¾" x 1½" walk. For
shrubs, trace pattern, page 135, onto
tracing paper; cut out. Using pattern, cut
two shrubs from wrappers.

5. Glue peppermint, door, windows, walk,
shrubs, straw candy wrappers, and foam
peanuts to house.

6. Use dimensional paint to outline and
add detail lines to peppermint, door,
windows, walk, and shrubs. Use stencil
brush to apply snow paint to desired areas.

TRIPLE-YOUR-FUN SNOWMEN

*T*riple your holiday fun with our trio of holiday snowmen! Fashioned around empty fabric bolts, these no-sew snowmen have facial features made out of bottle caps, buttons, and stones. Batting and plush felt give the snow guys their snuggly appeal.

FABRIC BOLT SNOWMEN

Recycled items: cardboard fabric bolts (23¼" long), buttons for vest and eyes, plastic bottle caps, and rocks for mouth

For each snowman, you will also need a hot glue gun, batting, 24" x 30" piece of plush white felt, fabric for vest and hat, craft glue, 2" dia. pom-pom, black sewing thread, 3" x 6" piece of black felt for bow tie, and orange spray paint.

Use hot glue for all gluing unless otherwise indicated.

1. For each snowman, glue several layers of batting to one side (front) of bolt for padding.
2. Place bolt front side down on plush felt. Wrap top and bottom ends of felt to back of bolt; glue in place. Overlapping side edges at back, wrap plush felt around bolt; glue in place.

3. Follow *Making Patterns*, page 156, to make a full-size vest pattern, page 136. Using pattern, cut two vest pieces (one in reverse) from fabric. Press edges ¼" to wrong side; use craft glue to glue in place. Overlapping pieces ½" at front, glue vest to snowman. Glue buttons to vest.
4. For hat, cut a 10" x 24" piece from fabric. Matching right sides, glue short edges together. Press one edge 1¾" to wrong side. Baste along opposite edge.

Pull thread ends to gather; tie to secure. Turn hat right side out; turn up cuff 1½". Place hat on snowman; glue to secure. Glue pom-pom to top of hat.
5. Knot a length of thread around center of felt piece to form bow tie. Glue tie to snowman.
6. For nose, paint bottle cap orange. Glue nose, buttons, and rocks to snowman for face.

DO-IT-YOURSELF FRAME

*F*or a practical way to feature your favorite seasonal snapshots, craft a do-it-yourself "frame" in a jiffy! This photo holder, which is wide enough to stand on its own, is created by spraying a plastic produce container gold, then attaching a photo and festive trims.

PRODUCE CONTAINER FRAME

Recycled items: plastic produce container, gold trim, and ribbon

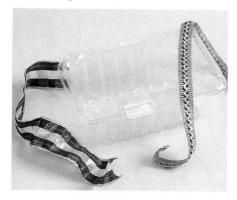

You will also need gold spray paint, photograph, glue stick, hot glue gun, and gold charms.

Use hot glue for all gluing unless otherwise indicated.

1. Paint container gold; allow to dry.
2. Trim photograph to fit top of container; use glue stick to glue in place. Glue trim around edge of photograph. Glue charms to trim.
2. Tie a 20" length of ribbon into a bow; arrange and glue to frame.

FANTASYLAND TOPIARY

A candy lover's delight, our "peppermint" topiary brings a fantasyland touch to your home. A coffee can serves as the base for the cellophane-wrapped "candy," which is made from painted foam plates.

PEPPERMINT TOPIARY

Recycled items: coffee can and white foam plates

You will also need grey spray primer; green spray paint; $2^1/_2$"w red-and-white striped ribbon; hot glue gun; floral foam; red acrylic paint; paintbrush; foam brush; craft glue; iridescent glitter; 20" of $^1/_2$" dia. wooden dowel; cellophane; 8" of craft wire; 1 yd. of 1"w white wired ribbon; white, red, and green curling ribbon; and red shredded paper.

Allow primer, paint, and glue to dry after each application unless otherwise indicated. Use hot glue for all gluing unless otherwise indicated.

1. Spray can with primer, then green paint.
2. Measure around coffee can; cut a length of striped ribbon the determined measurement. Glue ribbon around can.
3. Fill can with floral foam.

4. Paint a peppermint candy design on back of each plate. Use foam brush to apply craft glue over painted design on each plate. While glue is still wet, generously sprinkle glitter over glue. Shake gently to remove excess glitter.
5. With one end of dowel between plates, glue plates together. Wrap cellophane around plates and gather excess around dowel; secure with wire. Tie wired ribbon into a bow around gathers. Tie several lengths of curling ribbon into a bow. Curl ribbon ends. Glue curling ribbon bow to knot of wired ribbon bow.
6. Insert dowel into floral foam in can. Arrange shredded paper over foam.

JOLLY OLD ELF

Our holly-jolly shelf-sitter, a ready reminder of the festive season, adds Yuletide merriment to a cozy corner, shelf, or tabletop! A spray-painted plastic produce container forms Santa's body, and torn-fabric strips are attached for his arms and legs.

PRODUCE CONTAINER SANTA

Recycled items: plastic produce container, fabrics, poster board, ribbon, and pull tab

You will also need red spray paint, tracing paper, spray adhesive, hot glue gun, black permanent fine-point marker, and ¹/₂" dia. white pom-pom.

1. Paint container red; allow to dry.
2. For shirt, trace around top of container on wrong side of fabric; cut out.
3. For head, trace patterns, page 135, onto tracing paper. Using patterns, cut face, hat, hat trim, beard, and mustache from fabrics.
4. Apply spray adhesive to wrong sides of fabric pieces; smooth pieces separately onto poster board. Cut shirt and head shapes from fabric-covered poster board.

5. Overlapping as necessary, glue head shapes together. Use marker to draw eyes on face. Glue shirt, then head to top of container.
6. For belt, measure around container; add 3". Cut a length of ribbon the determined measurement. Glue one end of ribbon around center post of pull tab.

Wrap ribbon around container. Thread remaining end through pull tab. Glue belt to shirt to secure.
7. Tear two 1" x 8" fabric strips for arms and two 1" x 12" fabric strips for legs. Knot center and each end of each strip. Glue arms and legs to container and pom-pom to hat.

SNOWY DOORMAN

*S*et the tone for holiday fun right at your doorstep with our one-man welcoming committee. Wrapped in a "recycled" muffler and mittens (just like a traditional snowman), this snow buddy is crafted using scraps of vinyl flooring. He's embellished with tree limb arms, bottle cap eyes, and a smile made with stones.

VINYL FLOORING SNOWMAN

Recycled items: vinyl flooring scraps, two wide-mouth jar lid inserts, two metal bottle caps for eyes, rocks for mouth, $2^1/_2$' x 5' piece of cardboard (pieced as necessary), mittens, plastic bags, small tree limbs, and scarf

You will also need string; pencil; thumbtack; utility knife; tracing paper; white, orange, and black acrylic paint; natural sponge; black spray paint; paintbrushes; clear acrylic spray sealer; hot glue gun; nail; and jute twine.

Allow paint and sealer to dry after each application. Use utility knife to cut all vinyl pieces.

1. For head, tie one end of an 18" length of string to pencil. Insert thumbtack through string 6" from pencil, then into wrong side of vinyl. Draw circle on vinyl (Fig. 1); cut out. Repeat inserting thumbtack through string 9" and 12" from pencil to make two additional circles.

Fig. 1

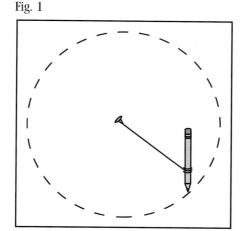

2. For hat, cut one $7^1/_2$" x 8" and one $2^1/_2$" x 12" piece from vinyl. Trace nose pattern, page 131, onto tracing paper; cut out. Draw around pattern on wrong side of vinyl; cut out.

3. Follow *Sponge Painting*, page 157, to paint wrong side of circles white. Spray paint wrong side of hat pieces, jar lid inserts, and eyes black. For buttons, use white paint to paint "buttonholes" and "stitches" on jar lid inserts. Paint nose orange. Use black paint to add details to nose. Apply sealer to all pieces.

4. Glue circles together to make snowman. Glue hat to top of head. Draw around snowman on cardboard; cut out $^1/_2$" inside drawn line.

5. For hanger assembly, use nail to punch ten holes in hat of cardboard snowman (Fig. 2). Lace a 1 yd. length of twine through holes. Tie ends of twine together. Glue cardboard snowman to back of vinyl snowman.

Fig. 2

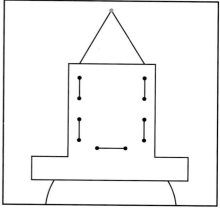

6. Glue eyes, nose, and mouth to head for face. Glue buttons to body.

7. Stuff mittens with plastic bags. Insert one limb into each mitten. Tie a length of twine around wrist of mitten to secure. For arms, glue limbs to back of body. Cut two 3" x 5" pieces from vinyl; glue one piece across each limb on back of body to secure.

8. Tie scarf around neck.

JAZZY SNOWMAN

When you need an extra-special delivery for holiday treats, you can count on our capricious snowman! To bring this whimsical character to life, we jazzed up a spray-painted soda bottle with craft foam cutouts.

SODA BOTTLE SNOWMAN

Recycled item: two-liter plastic bottle

You will also need craft knife, masking tape, white and black spray paint, craft glue, clothespins, push pin, heavy-duty thread, two 3" dia. red pom-poms, tracing paper, and orange and black craft foam.

Allow paint and glue to dry after each application.

1. Mark around bottle 7" from bottom. Use craft knife to cut away top along mark.
2. For handle, cut a 1" x 13" strip from top section of bottle. Trim each end to a point.
3. Wrap handle and cover top edge of container with masking tape.
4. Spray paint outside of bottle white and handle black.
5. Glue one end of handle to each side of container near top edge; secure with clothespins until dry. Use push pin to punch four holes through each end of handle into bottle (Fig. 1). Reinforce each end of handle by stitching an "X" through holes in handle and bottle. For ear muffs, glue a pom-pom over each end of handle.
6. For face, trace nose pattern, page 132, onto tracing paper; cut out. Draw around nose on orange craft foam; cut out. Rough cut two 1¼" circles for eyes and six ¾" circles for mouth from black craft foam. Glue shapes to bottle.

Fig. 1

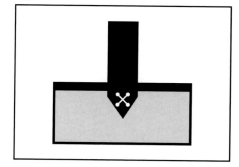

REINDEER PALS

*T*aking a rest from their North Pole duties, Donder and Blitzen and their buddies light up your mantel with a sleighful of fun. Painted bottle caps and twigs add animated appeal to reindeer heads crafted from stuffed paper bags.

PAPER BAG REINDEER TEAM

Recycled items: poster board, eight metal bottle caps, lunch-size brown paper bags, plastic bags, eight twist ties, and twigs
You will also need tracing paper, brown and black permanent fine-point markers, spray primer, white and red spray paint, hot glue gun, gravel, eight plastic resealable sandwich bags, and ribbon.

Allow primer and paint to dry after each application.

1. Trace eyes pattern, page 144, onto tracing paper; cut out. Draw around pattern sixteen times on poster board. Use black marker to color eyes; cut out.
2. For each nose, spray bottle caps with primer, then red paint.

3. For each reindeer, glue two eyes and one nose to one side of each bag. Use black marker to draw mouth on each bag.
4. Place a small amount of gravel in sandwich bag. Place sandwich bag in paper bag. Lightly stuff bag with plastic bags to three inches from top.
5. Gather top of bag; secure with twist tie.
6. For antlers, paint twigs white. Glue antlers to back of reindeer.
7. For each name tag, cut a 2$\frac{1}{2}$" x 5" piece from paper bag. Use brown marker to write name and draw "wood" accents on tag.
8. Arrange reindeer and tags on mantel. Wrapping ribbon around gathers of each reindeer, weave ribbon between reindeer.

TABLE WRAP-UPS

*F*or a holiday table that's merry and bright, whip up place mats and napkin rings featuring the festive patterns of your favorite Christmas wrap. It takes just minutes to create table settings by adhering wrapping paper to brown bags and poster board.

PAPER BAG PLACE SETTINGS

Recycled items: large brown paper bag, wrapping paper, poster board, ribbon, artificial greenery, and small glass ornaments

You will also need decorative-edge craft scissors, spray adhesive, black permanent fine-point marker, and a hot glue gun.

1. For each place mat, cut an 11¹/₄" x 15¹/₂" piece from paper bag. Using craft scissors, cut a 10¹/₂" x 14³/₄" piece from wrapping paper.
2. Apply spray adhesive to wrong side of wrapping paper. Center and smooth paper piece on bag piece.
3. Use marker to add "stitches" around place mat.
4. For each napkin ring, cut a 1¹/₂" x 5¹/₂"

piece from poster board and a 3" x 5¹/₂" piece from wrapping paper.
5. Overlapping ends ¹/₂", glue short ends of poster board together. Apply spray adhesive to wrong side of wrapping paper.

Center and smooth paper around ring; fold edges to inside of ring.
6. Tie ribbon into a bow around ring. Glue greenery and ornaments to bow.

SEASON'S GREETINGS TOWER

*W*rap up a unique season's greeting for one and all with our eye-catching Yuletide tower! Created with gift-wrapped cardboard boxes, this festive display is highlighted with letters crafted from gold poster board.

CARDBOARD BOX "NOEL"

Recycled items: four cardboard boxes (each large enough to accommodate a 6" x 8" design on one side) and assorted wrapping paper

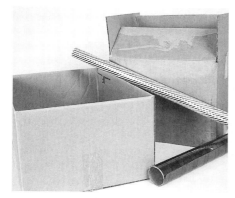

You will also need tape, gold poster board, hot glue gun, and 2"w ribbon.

1. Wrap each box like a package. Stack and glue boxes together.
2. Cut seven 1¹/₂" x 8" A strips, five 1¹/₂" x 6" B strips, and one 1¹/₂" x 4" C strip from poster board. Refer to Fig. 1 to center and glue one letter to each box.

Fig. 1

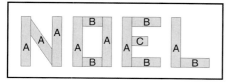

3. Cut a length of ribbon long enough to wrap around boxes. Glue ends together on top of boxes. Follow *Making a Bow*, page 157, to make a bow with twelve 9" loops, a center loop, and two 4" streamers. Glue bow to top of boxes.

GOOD "TIE-DINGS"

Who would ever imagine that formerly favorite neckties could be "recycled" into a handsome patchwork stocking! Appliquéd shapes, decorative embroidery, and beads accent pieces assembled in crazy-patch fashion.

Recycled items: neckties

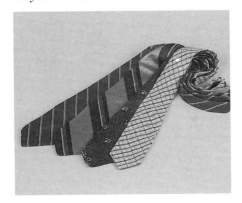

You will also need paper-backed fusible web, two 12" x 20" pieces of muslin, tracing paper, embroidery floss and beads to coordinate with neckties, ecru felt, and a safety pin.

Match right sides and raw edges and use a ¹/₄" seam allowance for all sewing unless otherwise indicated. Refer to Embroidery Stitches, page 158, to work decorative stitches.

1. Disassemble ties and remove lining; press tie fabrics. Cut a 2¹/₂" x 7" piece for hanger and a 2¹/₂" x 18" piece for bow from tie fabric. Using heart pattern, page 138, follow Steps 1 - 4 of *Making Appliqués,* page 157, to make one heart appliqué from tie fabric.

2. Fuse web onto wrong sides of remaining tie fabrics. For crazy-quilt pieces, cut desired shapes from fused fabric. Overlapping edges ¹/₄" and trimming to fit, arrange shapes on each muslin piece; fuse in place.

3. Extending lines of pattern as indicated, trace pattern, page 138, onto tracing paper. Draw a second line ¹/₄" outside traced line along sides and bottom of stocking.

4. Matching right sides and raw edges, place fused muslin pieces together. Using pattern, cut stocking front and stocking back from fused muslin pieces.

5. Fuse appliqué on stocking front. Work decorative stitches and add beads to stocking front, being careful not to stitch beads in seam allowance.

6. Leaving top edge open, sew stocking front and stocking back together. Clip curves and turn right side out.

7. For cuff, cut a 5" x 10¹/₂" piece of felt. Sew short ends together to form a tube. Matching wrong sides and raw edges, fold cuff in half. Matching raw edges and cuff seam to heel seam, place cuff inside stocking; sew in place. Fold cuff down over top of stocking.

8. For hanger, matching right sides and long edges, fold fabric piece for hanger in half. Sew along long edge. Turn right side out. Matching short, raw edges of hanger with heel seam of stocking, sew hanger to stocking.

9. For bow, matching right sides and long edges, press fabric piece for bow in half. Trim ends of strip diagonally. Sew raw edges together, leaving one end open for turning. Clip corners diagonally, turn right side out, and press. Blindstitch opening closed. Tie into a bow. Work decorative stitches at each end of bow. Use safety pin on wrong side of stocking to pin bow to stocking cuff.

trim the
TREE

*O*odles of enchanting ornaments transform your tree into a fantasyland of holiday fun. This year, dress your evergreen with festive finery made from items earmarked for the recycling bin! Bring back images of old-fashioned Christmases with a "popcorn" garland made out of packing peanuts. Then sprinkle the branches with rustic pinecone angels and clever Santa ornaments made with food cans. Top off the tree with a brown paper bag snowman, and piece together flannel shirts for a cozy tree skirt. You'll also find keepsake ornament containers made from Christmas card-embellished shoe boxes so you can store your treasures in style. Whatever your fancy, Trim the Tree is filled with appealing ideas to make your tree a one-of-a-kind attraction!

SNOW FLURRIES

*S*uper simple to make, our light and lacy snowflakes will cover your tree with a blizzard of fun. To craft these wintry wonders, trace the delicate shapes on foam food trays, then cut out with a craft knife and add a button center.

FOAM TRAY SNOWFLAKES

Recycled items: foam food trays and buttons

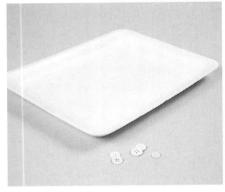

You will also need tracing paper, pencil, craft knife, cutting mat, craft glue, and clear nylon thread.

1. Trace pattern, page 128, onto tracing paper; cut out. For each snowflake, use pencil to draw around pattern on tray. Use craft knife to cut snowflake from tray.
2. Glue button to center of snowflake.
3. For hanger, knot ends of a 10" length of clear thread together; glue to snowflake.

"FASHIONABLE" STAR

When favorite ties have lost their luster as fashion accessories, just turn them into a star attraction on your holiday tree! Beads and decorative stitching add pizzazz to our patchwork creation.

NECKTIE STAR ORNAMENT

Recycled items: neckties

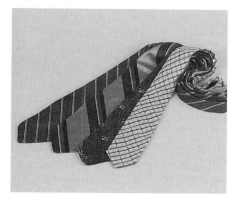

You will also need paper-backed fusible web, two 7" squares of muslin, tracing paper, embroidery floss and beads to coordinate with neckties, fiberfill, large-eye needle, and 12" of ¹/₁₆"w satin ribbon.

Match right sides and raw edges and use a ¹/₄" seam allowance for all sewing unless otherwise indicated. Refer to Embroidery Stitches, page 158, to work decorative stitches.

1. Disassemble ties and remove lining; press tie fabrics. Fuse web onto wrong sides of tie fabrics. For crazy-quilt pieces, cut desired shapes from fused fabric. Overlapping edges ¹/₄" and trimming to fit, arrange shapes on each muslin piece; fuse in place.
2. Trace pattern, page 139, onto tracing paper. Matching right sides and raw edges, place fused muslin pieces together. Using pattern, cut star front and star back from fused muslin pieces.
3. Work decorative stitches and add beads to right side of star front, being careful not to stitch beads in seam allowance.
4. Leaving an opening for turning, sew star front and star back together. Clip corners and points. Turn right side out. Stuff star with fiberfill; blindstitch opening closed.
5. For hanger, use needle to thread ribbon through point of star. Tie ends together into a bow.

WINTER JUGGLER

*J*uggling a flurry of activities is the key to holiday fun, as our snow buddy readily reminds us. This happy-go-lucky snowball juggler is easily crafted from brown paper bags, twigs, fabric, and buttons.

PAPER BAG SNOWMAN

Recycled items: brown paper bag, two small twigs for arms, plastic bags, and fabric for scarf

You will also need a 5" x 9" piece of white fabric, paper-backed fusible web, black permanent fine-point marker, orange chenille stem, two ³/₈" dia. black buttons for eyes, three ⁷/₁₆" dia. black buttons, hot glue gun, 34" length of medium-gauge craft wire, drawing compass, and white dimensional paint.

1. Using pattern, page 147, follow *Making Appliqués*, page 157, to make one snowman appliqué from white fabric.
2. Cut two 6" x 12" pieces from paper bag. Fuse appliqué to center on unprinted side of one paper bag piece. Use marker to draw "stitches" around snowman.
3. Place paper pieces printed sides

together and cut out snowman ¹/₄" outside drawn stitches. With twigs between layers and leaving an opening for stuffing, glue edges of front and back pieces together. Stuff snowman with plastic bag; glue opening closed.
4. For nose, cut a 3" length from chenille stem; twist into a spiral. Glue eyes, buttons, and nose to snowman. Tear a ³/₄" x 10" piece from fabric for scarf. Knot around neck of snowman; glue to secure.

5. For hanger, curl 6" of each end of wire around pencil. Bend wire to form a loop between ends. Twist ends around snowman arms; glue to secure.
6. For snowflakes, use compass to draw six ³/₄" dia. circles on paper bag; cut out. Use dimensional paint to draw snowflakes on each circle. Use marker to draw "stitches" on each snowflake.
7. Glue two snowflakes together over wire. Repeat with remaining snowflakes.

NATURALLY CHARMING

*N*ature lovers will appreciate this backyard beauty of a Christmas angel! Our naturally charming cherub is crowned with an acorn cap "halo" and displays twiggy "wings" on her pinecone body.

PINECONE ANGEL

Recycled items: acorn, pinecone, twigs, and ribbon

You will also need a black permanent fine-point marker, hot glue gun, and jute twine.

1. For head, use marker to draw eyes on acorn just below cap. Glue head to pointed end of pinecone.
2. For wings, use twine to tie four 4¹/₄" long twigs together at center. Glue to back of pinecone.
3. Tie a 6¹/₂" length of ribbon into a bow; glue to neck of angel.

NOSTALGIC CARD ORNAMENTS

*S*parkling with glitter and accented with ribbon rosebuds, your most beautiful Christmas cards become miniature works of art! Create these exquisite ornaments by embellishing card cutouts with paper doilies, charms, and scraps of pretty ribbon and trim.

GLITTERED CARD ORNAMENTS

Recycled items: Christmas cards, poster board, gold ribbon, trim, and artificial greenery

You will also need a foam brush, craft glue, glitter, paper doilies, hot glue gun, ribbon roses, gold buttons, and gold charms.

Use hot glue for all gluing unless otherwise indicated.

1. For each ornament, cut desired motif from card. Draw around motif on poster board; cut out.
2. Mix one part craft glue with one part water. Use foam brush to apply glue to areas of ornament where glitter is desired. While glue is still wet, generously sprinkle ornament with glitter. Shake gently to remove excess glitter.

3. Cut pieces from doily to frame ornament; glue to back of ornament. For hanger, glue ends of a 6" length of ribbon to back of ornament. Glue poster board to back of ornament.

4. Beginning and ending at top, glue trim along edge of ornament. Tie ribbon into bows. Glue bows, roses, buttons, charms, and greenery to ornament.

SPARKLING REFLECTIONS

*A*dd *a fantasyland feel to your Christmas decor by transforming old ornaments into shimmering treasures! To achieve the shiny effect, simply glue foil gum wrappers to an ornament and embellish with acrylic jewels.*

GUM WRAPPER-COVERED ORNAMENTS

Recycled items: ornaments and foil gum wrappers

You will also need foam brush, craft glue, assorted acrylic jewels, and gold dimensional paint.

1. Remove cap and wire from each ornament.
2. Use foam brush to apply glue to wrong side of wrappers. Smooth wrappers onto ornaments, overlapping as necessary; allow to dry.
3. To attach each jewel, squeeze a dot of paint the same size as jewel onto ornament. Press jewel into paint; allow to dry.
4. Replace caps and wires.

PATCHWORK TREE SKIRT

*T*he snuggly comfort of
flannel gives a country feel to
this tree skirt. It's quick and easy
to assemble squares of plaid
flannel (cut from shirts) into
a skirt featuring fringe trim
and button accents.

FLANNEL SHIRT TREE SKIRT

Recycled items: flannel shirts and
assorted buttons

You will also need string, fabric marking
pen, thumbtack, seam ripper, two
3" x 3³/₄ yd. strips of fabric for fringe
(pieced as necessary), and embroidery
floss.

Match right sides and raw edges and
use a ¹/₄" seam allowance for all sewing.

1. Wash, dry, and press all fabrics.
2. Cut sixty-four 6" squares from shirts.
Sew eight squares into a row; repeat to
make a total of eight rows. Matching
seams, sew rows together along long
edges.
3. Fold square in half from top to bottom
and again from left to right. Tie one end
of string to fabric marking pen. Insert
thumbtack through string 22" from pen.
Insert thumbtack in fabric; keeping string
taut, mark cutting line (Fig. 1). Repeat to
mark inner cutting line, inserting
thumbtack through string 1¹/₂" from pen.

Fig. 1

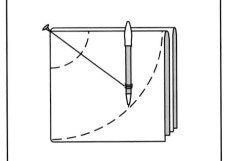

4. Cutting through all layers of fabric, cut
out skirt along marked lines; unfold.
5. For opening at back of skirt, use seam
ripper to open one seam from inner
circle to outer edge. Press edges ¹/₄" to
wrong side and sew in place.
6. For fringe, matching wrong side to
right side, baste strips together along one
long edge. Clip strips at ¹/₂" intervals
along opposite edge to ¹/₂" from basting
thread. Pull basting thread, gathering
fringe to fit outer edge of skirt. With right
sides together, sew fringe to skirt. Press
seam allowance to wrong side.
7. Tying floss at front, sew buttons to skirt
as desired.

HEIRLOOM ORNAMENTS

*G*ive your tree a little glamour by turning outdated jewelry into attention-getting ornaments. Discover how fun and easy it is to artistically arrange vintage pins, pendants, and other pieces on fabric-covered foam balls. You'll be amazed at the one-of-a-kind decorations you can create!

VINTAGE JEWELRY ORNAMENTS

Recycled items: fabric, costume jewelry, gold cord, and ribbon

For each ornament, you will also need drawing compass, tracing paper, thread, half of a 3" dia. plastic foam ball, and a hot glue gun.

1. For pattern, use compass to draw a 9" dia. circle on tracing paper. Using pattern, cut circle from fabric. Press raw edge of circle 1/4" to wrong side. Using a double strand of thread, work a *Running Stitch*, page 159, along pressed edge.
2. Center foam piece, round side down on wrong side of fabric circle. Pull ends of thread to gather fabric around foam piece; knot thread ends together.
3. Covering fabric edges, arrange and glue jewelry to fabric on flat side of ball.

Glue cord around edge of ornament. Glue additional jewelry to bottom of ornament.
4. For hanger, knot ends of a 5" length of cord together. Glue knot to top of ornament. Tie ribbon into a bow; glue to knot of hanger.

BRILLIANT SANTA

*J*ust in case his lead reindeer's nose refuses to shine, this adorable Santa has a spare light for his annual midnight sleigh ride! The jolly old elf is made from a painted light bulb accented with a sock hat and a beard of packing peanuts.

ROUND BULB SANTA

Recycled items: round vanity light bulb, child-size red sock, foam packing peanuts, ribbon, and artificial greenery

You will also need tracing paper; transfer paper; white, pink, red, brown, and black acrylic paint; paintbrushes; craft wire; wire cutters; hot glue gun; and a 1" dia. pom-pom.

1. Trace eyes pattern, page 137, onto tracing paper. With base of bulb at top, use transfer paper to transfer eyes to bulb. Paint face.
2. Wrap one end of a 10" length of wire around base of bulb; glue to secure.
3. For hat, thread wire through toe end of sock. Fold cuff up twice and arrange on head; glue to secure. Glue pom-pom to top of hat.

4. Glue foam peanuts to face for beard. Cut three foam peanuts in half lengthwise. Glue one piece to face below nose for mustache. Glue four pieces over edge of beard at chin.
5. Tie ribbon into a bow. Glue bow and greenery to hat. Bend wire to form hanger.

PEACEFUL MESSENGER

A messenger of peace
and harmony, this Christmas
dove bears glad tidings for all
your loved ones. The graceful
ornament, which also makes
a lovely package decoration,
is simple to make. Cut the
pattern pieces from a foam
tray, assemble, and highlight
with a gold leaf pen.

FOAM TRAY DOVE

Recycled items: white foam tray and a
Christmas card

You will also need tracing paper, black
permanent fine-point marker, craft knife,
cutting mat, craft glue, gold paint pen,
wire cutters, and medium-gauge
craft wire.

1. Trace dove and wing patterns,
page 140, onto tracing paper; cut out.
Use marker to draw around patterns on
foam tray.
2. Use craft knife to cut dove and wing
from foam tray. Use a pencil to make
indentations in feathers, body, and wings.
Position and glue wing to dove.
3. Use marker to add eye and paint pen
to add highlights along edges of dove.

4. Cut desired motif from Christmas card;
glue to beak of dove.

5. Glue a 7" length of wire to back of
dove. Bend wire to form hanger.

TWINKLING STAR GARLAND

*L*ike diamonds in the night, cutout stars twinkle merrily on our silvery garland. Clear plastic food containers and lids are decorated with glitter and dimensional paint to produce the sparkling tree trim.

PLASTIC LID STAR GARLAND

Recycled items: clear plastic food containers and opaque plastic lids

You will also need tracing paper, white dimensional paint, ¹/₈" dia. hole punch, foam brush, craft glue, clear glitter, silver chenille stems, and ¹/₂"w silver wired ribbon.

1. Trace pattern, page 140, onto tracing paper; cut out.
2. For clear stars, use pattern to cut desired number of stars from food containers. Use dimensional paint to outline each star; allow to dry. Punch one hole in one point of each star.
3. For frosted stars, use pattern to cut desired number of stars from opaque lids. Punch one hole in one point of two stars for garland ends. Punch one hole in two opposite points of remaining stars.
4. For each star, use foam brush to apply glue to entire star. While glue is still wet,

sprinkle with glitter; shake gently to remove excess glitter.
5. For garland, beginning and ending with stars for garland ends and connecting stars end-to-end, use chenille stems to connect frosted stars.

6. For each clear star, cut one 3¹/₂" length of chenille stem and one 12" length of silver ribbon. Thread one stem end through hole in star; twist to secure. Twist opposite end around garland between frosted stars. Tie ribbon into a bow around stem.

ANGELIC CHARM

A symbol of innocence and joy, our Christmas angel crowns your tree with charm. Fashioned from a sock-covered foam egg and a plastic soda bottle, this adorable cherub is decked out in stiffened doily wings and a plastic-lid halo!

SODA BOTTLE ANGEL

Recycled items: two-liter plastic bottle, adult-size white tube sock, rubber bands, ribbon, buttons, plastic lid, and a yellow foam food tray

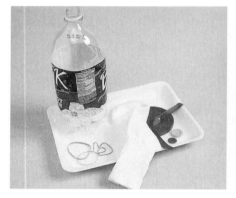

You will also need a hot glue gun; 2¹/₄" x 3" plastic foam egg; fabric; one 12" oval, one 9" dia., and two 6" dia. doilies; jute twine; two craft sticks; fabric stiffener; two straight pins with black heads; cosmetic blush; curly doll hair; gold spray paint; star-shaped cookie cutter; craft knife; cutting mat; Design Master® wood-tone spray; and a wired miniature garland.

Allow paint and wood-tone spray to dry after each application.

1. For body, cut 2" from bottom of bottle. Remove lid from bottle. Glue small end of egg to opening.

2. Place body head first in sock. Wrap edge of sock to inside of bottle; glue to secure.

3. For dress, cut a 12" x 24" piece of fabric. Overlapping ¹/₂", glue short edges together to form a tube. Place tube over bottle. Gather fabric at neck with rubber band.

4. For apron, gather 9" dia. doily at front of neck; secure under rubber band. Tie twine, then ribbon into a bow around neck, covering rubber band. Glue button to bow.

5. For each arm, wrap one craft stick with one 6" dia. doily; glue to secure. Glue arms to angel.

6. For wings, baste across width at center of oval doily. Pull threads to gather; tie tightly to secure. Follow manufacturer's instructions to stiffen wings. Glue wings to back of angel.

7. For face, insert pins in head for eyes and apply blush for cheeks.

8. Glue doll hair to head. For halo, paint lid gold; glue to back of head.

9. For garland, press cookie cutter into foam tray. Use craft knife to cut out star and lightly score star ¹/₈" in from edge. Lightly spray star with wood-tone spray.

10. Wrap garland around 18" of twine. Glue star to center of garland. Glue button to star. Tie one end of twine around each arm.

HOLIDAY "LIGHTS"

*T*ransform clear plastic food containers into oversize "tree lights" quicker than Santa can give a wink of his eye and a twist of his head! Our whimsical garland, complete with its own "electrical plug," adds sparkle to your decor.

FOOD CONTAINER "LIGHT" STRAND

Recycled items: large clear plastic food containers

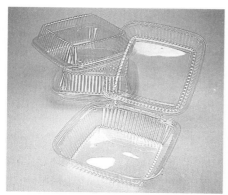

You will also need black dimensional paint, craft glue, foam brush, white tissue paper, assorted colors of acrylic paint, paintbrushes, push pin, floral wire, wire cutters, and 40" of ¼" dia. green cord.

1. Using dimensional paint and patterns, page 132, trace six bulbs, one plug, and one socket onto flat areas of plastic containers; allow to dry.
2. Mix one part glue with one part water. Use foam brush to apply glue mixture to back of plastic over designs. Place tissue paper over glue and smooth in place; allow to dry.
3. For each paint color, mix one part acrylic paint with one part water. Paint

tissue side of each design as desired; allow to dry.
4. Cut out each design.
5. Use push pin to make a hole at top of each bulb. Use wire to attach bulbs to cord.
6. Glue plug and socket to opposite ends of cord.

SANTA'S CANDY CUPS

*W*hat clever ornaments! These Santa-embellished candy holders make great party favors or package decorations that can be refilled and hung on the tree. Assembly is simple: just paint small cans, attach fabric with spray adhesive, and finish with a jolly old elf accent made with fused fabric and felt!

MINI CAN SANTA CUPS

Recycled items: small cans (we used 9-oz. tomato paste cans), fabric, assorted buttons, and ribbon

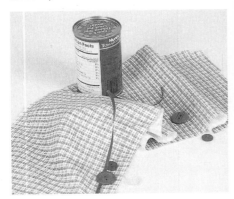

You will also need white spray primer, red spray paint, pinking shears, spray adhesive, paper-backed fusible web, white and green felt, hot glue gun, black permanent fine-point marker, white and red dimensional paint, hammer, and nail.

Allow primer and paint to dry after each application.

1. For each ornament, spray can with primer, then red paint.
2. Measure height of can. Measure around can; add ¹/₂". Use pinking shears to cut a piece from fabric the determined measurements.

3. Apply spray adhesive to wrong side of fabric. Overlapping ends at back, smooth fabric around can.
4. Using patterns, page 141, follow *Making Appliqués*, page 157, to make mustache, beard, and hat trim appliqués from white felt and hat and face appliqués from fabric. Arrange and fuse appliqués on green felt. Leaving a ¹/₈" border, use pinking shears to trim around Santa. Glue button to hat.

5. Use marker to draw eyes and mouth on face, white dimensional paint to draw eyebrows and add eye highlights, and red dimensional paint to make dot for nose. Glue Santa to can front.
6. For handle, use hammer and nail to punch a hole in each side of can. Cut a 12" length of ribbon. Working from inside of can, thread one end of ribbon through each hole in can. Thread a button onto each ribbon end; knot ribbon ends to secure.

"POPCORN" GARLAND

Revive the simple pleasures of long-ago Christmases with our homespun garland. Inspired by old-fashioned strings of popcorn, this festive strand is a cinch to make with easy-to-find packaging materials. Just alternate popcorn-shaped packing peanuts with painted foam "gumdrops" that are "sugar coated" with clear glitter.

PACKING PEANUTS GARLAND

Recycled items: smooth foam packing peanuts, buttons, and white foam popcorn-shaped packing peanuts

You will also need assorted colors of acrylic paint, paintbrushes, foam brush, craft glue, clear glitter, 5 yds. of $1/16$"w ribbon, 7 yds. of $3/8$"w ribbon, fifteen artificial greenery sprigs, and a low-temperature glue gun.

1. For gumdrops, cut smooth packing peanuts in half (Fig. 1). Paint halves desired colors; allow to dry.

Fig. 1

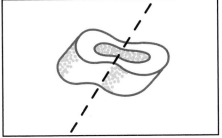

2. Use foam brush to apply craft glue to gumdrops. While glue is still wet, sprinkle gumdrops with glitter; shake gently to remove excess glitter. Allow to dry.

3. Knot $1/16$"w ribbon 11" from one end. Leaving 11" at opposite end and beginning and ending with a button, thread buttons, "popcorn," and gumdrops onto ribbon. Knot opposite end to secure.

4. Cut $3/8$"w ribbon into fifteen 16" lengths. Tie each length into a bow around a stem of greenery. Use low-temperature glue gun to glue greenery to garland.

SIMPLY STARRY

*C*hristmas dreams are sure to come true when you make a wish upon this simply charming star! Adorable on your tree or as a package accent, the star can be made in a twinkling. Just glue drinking straw segments together, spray paint, and embellish with seasonal frills.

DRINKING STRAW STARS

Recycled items: drinking straws and ribbon

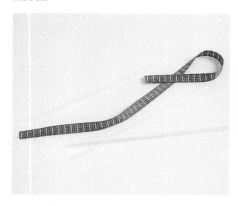

You will also need a low-temperature glue gun, red spray paint, 9mm liberty bell, and clear nylon thread.

1. For each star, cut five $5^{1}/_{2}$" lengths from straws.
2. Glue straws into a star shape (Fig. 1).

Fig. 1

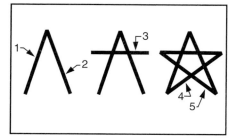

3. Paint star red; allow to dry.
4. Tie a 19" length of ribbon into a bow. Glue bow and bell to star. Arrange and glue streamers to star.

5. For hanger, tie an 8" length of thread through top point of star.

FESTIVE PHOTOS

*O*ur festive photo "frames" will turn your tree into a holiday gallery of snapshots. These cozy country ornaments are actually mayonnaise jar lids covered with fabric, trim, and ribbon scraps.

JAR LID PHOTO ORNAMENTS

Recycled items: jar lids, fabric, trim, and ribbon

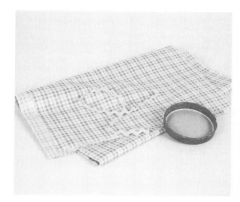

You will also need spray adhesive, photograph, glue stick, 6mm jingle bells, and a hot glue gun.

1. For each ornament, draw around lid on wrong side of fabric. Cut out fabric circle just inside drawn line. Apply spray adhesive to wrong side of circle; smooth onto top of lid.
2. Cut desired image from photograph. Using glue stick, center and glue to lid.
3. Trimming to fit, hot glue trim around side of lid.
4. Tie an 8" length of ribbon into a bow. Hot glue bow at top of ornament; glue bell to knot of bow.
5. For hanger, hot glue ends of a 6" length of ribbon together at top of ornament.

*F*or a rollicking good time, set this lively combo of snow creatures loose on your holiday tree! Created using crushed soda cans covered with textured snow paint, these endearing tree spirits get their engaging personalities from craft foam faces and whimsical limbs made from chenille stems and twigs.

FLATTENED CAN SNOWMEN

Recycled items: 12-oz. aluminum beverage cans, fabric, and twigs

You will also need white spray primer; textured snow paint; stencil brush; tracing paper; white, orange, red, and green craft foam; white and black felt; black permanent medium-point marker; pink colored pencil; low-temperature glue gun; white chenille stems; and items to decorate snowmen (we used miniature candy canes, liberty bells on ribbons, miniature artificial wreaths, jingle bells on embroidery floss, and miniature light garland).

Allow primer and paint to dry after each application.

1. For each snowman, remove tab from can. Use both hands to hold can with thumbs below top rim and opening. Using thumbs, press on can to bend top rim down. Turn can upside down and repeat to bend bottom of can in opposite direction. Step on can to flatten further (Fig. 1).

Fig. 1

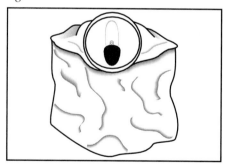

2. Spray can with one coat of primer. Use stencil brush to apply textured snow paint to can between rims.

3. Trace patterns, page 145, onto tracing paper; cut out. Use patterns to cut two boots from red or green craft foam, face from white craft foam, nose from orange craft foam, and two hat pieces from black felt.

4. Use marker to draw eyes and mouth on face. Use colored pencil to add cheeks. Glue nose to face.

5. Glue hat pieces together. Tear a $3/4$" x 5" strip of fabric. Overlapping ends at back, glue strip around hat.

6. For legs, cut two 3" lengths from twigs. Glue twigs to bottom of can.

7. For arms, cut a 1" x 10" piece of white felt. Matching long edges, center and glue felt piece around chenille stem. Loop each end to form hands. Cut felt-covered stem in half.

8. Arrange and glue face, hat, arms, and boots on snowman.

9. For scarf, tear a 1" x 14" strip from fabric; knot around neck of snowman.

10. Arrange and glue decorative items on snowman as desired.

BEAUTIFUL BAUBLE KEEPERS

*S*tore your holiday decorations in boxes that are as lovely as your cherished baubles! Accented with Christmas cards and gold trim, our containers are too pretty to put away while the ornaments are on the tree. So plan to keep the handy "recycled" shoe boxes close at hand as decorative holders for cards, wrapping supplies, stamps, and other Yuletide necessities.

SHOE BOX STORAGE CONTAINERS

Recycled items: shoe boxes, Christmas cards, and poster board

You will also need red or green spray paint, gold acrylic paint, natural sponge, straight-edge and decorative-edge craft scissors, craft glue, 1"w gold trim, red corrugated cardboard, black permanent medium-point marker, and a gold permanent fine-point marker.

Allow paint to dry after each application.

1. For each box, remove lid. Spray paint outside of lid and box desired color. Use gold paint and follow *Sponge Painting*, page 157, to paint sides of box.

2. Use craft scissors to cut desired motifs from cards. Overlapping as desired, glue motifs to lid.

3. Measure around sides of lid. Cut a length of gold trim the determined measurement; glue trim along bottom edge of lid.

4. Cut a $2^5/8$" x $5^1/2$" piece from cardboard for background and a 2" x 5" piece of poster board for label. Use black marker to write "Ornaments" on label. Use gold marker to add details along edges of label. Center and glue label to background. Center and glue label to lid.

CARD "MOSAICS"

*F*or charming tree trims or package decorations, create these stained-glass-look ornaments using your favorite Christmas cards. Cutting the cards into mosaic-type pieces and mounting them on card stock produces the "piecework" effect.

PIECED CARD ORNAMENTS

Recycled items: Christmas cards and gold cord

For each ornament, you will also need craft glue, card stock, ¹/₈" dia. hole punch, and an 8" length of metallic gold thread.

1. For each ornament, cut desired motif from card. Cut motif into pieces. Leaving ¹/₁₆" between pieces, arrange and glue pieces to card stock.
2. Leaving a ¹/₄" border around edges of motif, cut out ornament. If desired, glue ornament to a second piece of card stock and repeat.
3. Beginning and ending at top, glue gold cord around ornament. Tie a 10" length of cord into a bow; knot and trim ends. Glue bow to top of ornament.
4. For hanger, punch hole at top of ornament. Thread gold thread through hole; knot ends together.

"BRIGHT IDEA" SANTA

*B*righten up your tree with our jolly old elf ornament! He's easy to make from a large candle bulb and a section of wrapping paper tube. Santa's light bulb "beard" is enhanced with white dimensional paint, and a festive toddler-size sock serves as his signature cap.

CANDLE BULB SANTA

Recycled items: wrapping paper tube, 4" candle bulb, toddler-size sock, and artificial greenery

You will also need white, flesh, red, blue, and black acrylic paint; paintbrushes; tracing paper; transfer paper; hot glue gun; white dimensional paint; wire cutters; medium-gauge craft wire; and 1" dia. pom-pom.

Refer to Painting Techniques, page 156, to paint Santa face. Allow paint to dry after each application.

1. For head, cut a 2" length from wrapping paper tube; paint tube flesh. Trace pattern, page 135, onto tracing paper. Use transfer paper to transfer face to tube.

2. Use acrylic paint to paint face and cheeks and to add highlights to eyes and nose.
3. Covering bulb base, glue head to bulb. Use white dimensional paint to paint mustache and beard.
4. For hanger, cut a $4^{1}/_{2}$" length of wire. Glue one end to bulb base.
5. For hat, cut sock 6" from top (Fig. 1). Turn 6" piece wrong side out. Glue cut edges together. Turn right side out. Fold cuff of sock up $^{3}/_{4}$". Glue pom-pom to glued edges.

Fig. 1

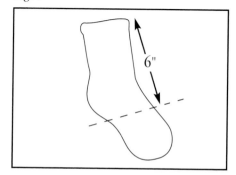

6. Threading hanger through sock, glue hat to tube. Glue stem of greenery inside cuff of hat. Bend wire to form hanger.

CLEVER CLAUS LIGHT CATCHERS

*M*ake your holidays merry
by decorating with our clever
Santa light catchers! They're easy
to construct — just paint tissue
paper that's glued to the back of
shapes cut from clear plastic
food containers.

FOOD CONTAINER SANTA ORNAMENTS

Recycled items: large clear plastic food
containers and scraps of satin ribbon

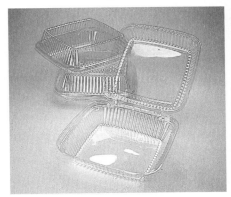

You will also need black dimensional
paint; craft glue; foam brush; white tissue
paper; white, flesh, red, green, and black
acrylic paint; paintbrushes; and ¹/₈" hole
punch.

1. For each ornament, using dimensional
paint and desired pattern, page 148 or
149, trace design onto flat areas of plastic
container.
2. Mix one part glue with one part water.
Use foam brush to apply glue mixture to
opposite side of plastic over design.
Smooth tissue paper over glue; allow
to dry.
3. For each color, mix one part acrylic
paint with one part water. Use acrylic
paint to paint design; allow to dry.

4. Cut out design.
5. For hanger, punch a hole in top of
ornament. Cut one 12" length of ribbon.

Fold ribbon in half. Thread fold through
hole. Insert ends of ribbon through loop;
pull tightly. Tie ends into a bow.

SUPER SWEATER TREE TRIMS

*W*rapped in the snuggly warmth of a well-loved sweater, our wintry ornaments add a cozy touch to your holiday decor. Super simple to craft, these no-sew ornaments are fashioned by tying sweater sleeves around foam balls.

SWEATER ORNAMENTS

Recycled items: sweater, yarn, and artificial greenery

You will also need a hot glue gun and 3" dia. plastic foam balls.

1. Measuring from finished edge, cut a 6" length from sweater sleeve.
2. Turn cut piece wrong side out; gather and glue cut edges together.
3. Turn piece right side out. Place ball in sleeve. Gather excess at top of ball; tie several 16" lengths of yarn into a bow around gathers to secure. Glue greenery to bow.

These ornaments have an "un-can-ny" resemblance to our favorite Christmas visitor! Crafted from food cans, our jolly Santas display sock hats and button noses.

BEARDED SANTA CANS

Recycled items: aluminum beverage can, can for head (we used 9-oz. tomato paste can), white shank-style buttons for nose and eyes, adult-size sock, and artificial greenery

You will also need white spray primer; tracing paper; white dimensional paint; hammer; nail; white, flesh, red, and black acrylic paint; natural sponge; hot glue gun; paintbrushes; craft wire; wire cutters; and a 1¹/₂" dia. pom-pom.

Allow primer and paint to dry after each application.

1. For each Santa, cut through opening and down to bottom of beverage can; cut away top and bottom of can. Flatten can piece.
2. Spray beverage can piece and can for head with primer.
3. Trace beard and mustache patterns,

"UN-CAN-NY" SANTAS

page 144, onto tracing paper; cut out. Draw around patterns on can piece; cut out. Use dimensional paint to add accents to beard and mustache.
4. For head, use hammer and nail to punch a hole in center of closed end of can. Follow *Sponge Painting*, page 157, to paint can flesh.
5. For eyes and nose, use wire cutters to remove shanks from buttons. Paint pupils black; add white highlights. Arrange and glue mustache, beard, eyes, and nose on head. Use dimensional paint to paint

eyebrows. Lightly apply red paint to cheeks and nose.
6. Cut a 6" length of craft wire. Bend one end into a small loop. Insert straight end up through hole in can; glue to secure.
7. For hat, cut an 8" piece from top of sock. Turn piece wrong side out. Gather cut edge and glue to secure; turn right side out. Glue pom-pom to gathered end.
8. Thread wire through sock. Fold cuff of sock up 1" and arrange on head; glue to secure. Glue greenery to hat. Bend wire to form hanger.

SIMPLY SUPER SNOW BUDDIES

*P*ut extra enjoyment into your winter weather activities with our fun-loving snow fellows. These juice-can-lid characters are especially adorable because of their delightful accessories — chenille stem ear muffs, a dapper felt hat, and toddler-sock hat and mufflers.

JUICE LID SNOW PALS

Allow primer, paint, and glue to dry after each application.

BASIC SNOWMAN ORNAMENT
Recycled item: lid from large frozen juice can

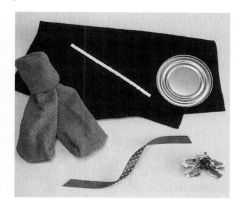

You will also need white spray primer; white, orange, red, and black acrylic paint; and paintbrushes.

1. Spray lid with two coats of primer.
2. Use acrylic paint to paint face.

SNOWMAN WITH STOCKING CAP
Recycled items: toddler-size green sock and a twist tie
You will also need Basic Snowman Ornament, thread, hot glue gun, 1" dia. green pom-pom, red-and-green striped toddler-size sock, and artificial snow.

1. For hat, cut cuff from green sock. Using a double strand of thread, work a *Running Stitch*, page 159, along cut edge. Gather stitches and tie thread ends together. Glue pom-pom over gathers. Fold opposite end $3/8$" to right side; glue hat to top of ornament.
2. For muffler, cut a $1^1/2$" x 6" piece from striped sock. Matching long edges, fold muffler in half. Forming a 2" dia. circle, loosely tie ends together. Insert "chin" of snowman into circle; glue to secure.
3. Lightly spray ornament with artificial snow.
4. For hanger, glue one end of twist tie to back of ornament; bend opposite end.

SNOWMAN WITH EAR MUFFS
Recycled items: toddler-size green sock and a twist tie
You will also need Basic Snowman Ornament, one $5^1/2$" length each of red and white chenille stems, hot glue gun, two 1" dia. red pom-poms, and artificial snow.

1. For ear muffs, twist chenille stems together; glue along top of ornament. Glue one pom-pom at each end of stems.
2. For muffler, cut a $1^1/2$"w piece from cuff of sock. Fold raw and finished edges $1/4$" to wrong side. Insert "chin" of snowman into opening of muffler; glue to secure.
3. Repeat Steps 3 and 4 of *Snowman with Stocking Cap* to finish ornament.

SNOWMAN WITH TOP HAT
Recycled items: $1^3/4$" x $3^1/2$" piece of black felt, $2^3/4$" of $3/4$"w ribbon, artificial greenery, $3/4$" x $9^3/4$" torn fabric strip, and a twist tie
You will also need Basic Snowman Ornament, tracing paper, hot glue gun, and artificial snow.

1. Trace pattern, page 134, onto tracing paper; cut out. Using pattern, cut hat from felt. Trimming to fit, glue ribbon along brim of hat; glue greenery to ribbon. Glue hat to top of ornament.
2. For muffler, tear a $3/4$" x $9^3/4$" strip from fabric. Forming a 2" dia. circle, loosely tie ends of fabric strip together. Insert "chin" of snowman into circle; glue to secure.
3. Repeat Steps 3 and 4 of *Snowman with Stocking Cap* to finish ornament.

great GIFTS

*Y*our search for great holiday gifts has just ended, and in a most unexpected place — your recycling bin! You'll be amazed at the assortment of homemade gifts from the heart that can be made with items you normally throw away. Inside these pages, you'll find a heavenly top made from a man's shirt, folksy frames crafted from foam food trays, and a fragrant candle tinted with melted crayons. We also show how to assemble twigs and photos into a rustic "family tree" that displays your clan's togetherness. From necklaces to hostess gifts and a memory album to a bath basket, Great Gifts contains a unique assortment of presents for your friends and loved ones!

YULETIDE MEMORY ALBUM

A favorite friend will love preserving precious Yuletide memories in this charming album. A posh appearance is achieved by rejuvenating an old album with batting-cushioned holiday fabric. Complete the look with a coordinating Christmas card in a gilded frame.

FRAMED CARD ALBUM

Recycled items: photo album with center rings, poster board, Christmas card, frame to fit on front of album, and ribbon

You will also need batting, hot glue gun, fabric, and spray adhesive.

1. Cut a piece of batting the same size as opened photo album. Glue batting to outside of album.
2. Cut a piece of fabric 1¹/₂" larger on all sides than opened album. Center opened album on wrong side of fabric piece.
3. Fold corners of fabric diagonally over corners of album; glue in place. Fold edges of fabric over side edges of album; glue in place. Fold edges of fabric over top and bottom edges of album, trimming fabric to fit ¹/₄" under binding hardware; glue in place.

4. Cut two 4"w fabric strips ¹/₂" shorter than height of album. Press ends of each strip ¹/₄" to wrong side. On inside of album, center and glue one strip along each side of binding hardware with one long edge of each strip tucked ¹/₄" under hardware.
5. To line inside of album, cut two pieces of poster board 1" smaller than front of album. Cut two pieces of fabric 2" larger than poster board pieces.

6. Apply spray adhesive to wrong side of one fabric piece. Center one poster board piece on wrong side of fabric piece. Fold corners of fabric piece diagonally over corners of poster board; smooth in place. Fold edges of fabric over edges of poster board; smooth in place. Repeat with remaining poster board and fabric.
7. Glue liners to insides of album.
8. Trim card to fit frame; mount in frame. Glue frame to front of album. Tie ribbon into a bow; glue to front of album.

FESTIVE FAVORS

*F*or old-fashioned Yuletide fun, craft these goodie-loaded Christmas favors! Embellished with cheery ribbon and gift wrap, a bunch of these treats make festive party favors. Create them in just minutes by decorating paper tubes with scraps of wrapping paper and adding a bundle of tulle-wrapped candies.

PAPER TUBE FAVORS

Recycled items: wrapping paper, toilet paper tubes, and narrow gold and red or green ribbons

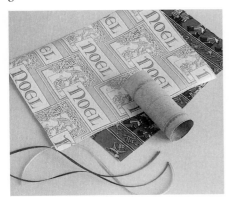

For each favor, you will also need spray adhesive, 11" x 12" piece of red or green tulle, and wrapped candies to fill favor.

1. Apply spray adhesive to wrong side of a 5$^1/_2$" x 6$^1/_2$" piece of wrapping paper.
2. With paper extending 1" at each end of tube, center and smooth paper around tube. Clipping as necessary, fold and press ends to inside of tube.
3. Overlapping short ends 1", fold tulle in half to form tube. Insert tulle tube in paper-covered tube.

4. Tie two 6" lengths of desired ribbons into a bow around one end of tulle tube. Fill favor with candy.

5. Tie two 6" lengths of desired ribbons into a bow around opposite end of tulle tube.

BATH BOUTIQUE

To create a soothing gift that shows you care, bundle sweet-smelling soaps and bath oil in a festive container. Use pretty ribbons and merry motifs from your Christmas card collection to personalize the fragrant accents.

CARD MOTIF BATH COLLECTION

DECORATED SOAPS
Recycled item: Christmas card
You will also need smooth bars of soap, craft glue, and a foam brush.

1. For each bar of soap, cut desired motif from card.
2. Mix one part glue with one part water.
3. Use foam brush to apply glue mixture to back of motif. Center motif on soap and smooth in place; allow to dry.
4. Apply glue mixture over motif; allow to dry.

BOTTLED BATH OIL
Recycled item: Christmas card
You will also need bottled bath oil, craft glue, drawing compass, gold tissue paper, and 1¹/₂"w plaid ribbon.

1. For bottle, cut desired motif from card.
2. Glue motif to bottle; allow to dry.

3. Use compass to draw a 5" dia. circle on tissue paper; cut out. Gather circle over top of bottle. Knot an 8" length of plaid ribbon around gathers.

TOWEL
You will need a hand towel, 1¹/₂"w plaid ribbon, hot glue gun, and a small safety pin.

1. Measure width of towel. Cut a length from ribbon the determined measurement. Centering ribbon on end of towel, topstitch long edges and zigzag over ends of ribbon on towel.
2. Cut one 3" length and one 12" length from plaid ribbon. Overlapping ends of 12" length ¹/₄", glue ribbon ends together to form a loop. Flatten loop with overlap at center back. Fold long edges of 3" ribbon length to center. Overlapping ends at back, wrap around center of loop; glue in place. Use safety pin to attach bow to towel.

BASKET
Recycled items: Christmas card and satin ribbon
You will also need decorated soaps, bottled bath oil, towel, basket (we used a sleigh-shaped basket), and a hole punch.

1. Arrange soaps, bath oil, and towel in basket.
2. For tag, cut desired motif from card. Punch hole in tag. Use ribbon to tie tag to basket.

HOLIDAY HOSTESS GIFT

A sparkling beverage takes on festive flair when the bottle is embellished with seasonal etched designs. It's surprisingly easy to add a fancy touch to this traditional hostess gift using glass etching cream and gold rub-on finish!

ETCHED WINE BOTTLE

Recycled items: wine bottle large enough to accommodate design, ribbon, Christmas card, and gold cord

You will also need clear Con-tact® paper, black permanent fine-point marker, craft knife, cutting mat, ¹/₄" hole punch, glass etching cream, gold rub-on metallic finish, paper towel, drawing compass, and gold tissue paper.

1. Measure around bottle. Cut a piece of Con-tact® paper 5¹/₂" by the determined measurement. For stencil, use marker to trace design, page 145, desired number of times onto paper side of Con-tact® paper. Use craft knife to carefully cut stencil along drawn lines. Punch holes inside lines of designs for ornaments.
2. Remove paper backing from stencil. Clipping edges as necessary to fit bottle, smooth stencil onto bottle.

3. Follow manufacturer's instructions to etch design onto bottle. Do not remove stencil.
4. Working with small sections at a time, rub gold finish over design; remove excess with a paper towel. Remove stencil from bottle.

5. Use compass to draw a 6" dia. circle on tissue paper; cut out. Gather circle over top of bottle; tie ribbon into a bow around gathers.
6. For tag, cut desired motif from card. Punch hole in tag. Use cord to tie tag to bottle.

F or a lovely remembrance, feature a Christmas card in a rustic woodland frame! These one-of-a-kind accent pieces are constructed using corrugated cardboard, festive embellishments, and twigs from your own backyard.

TWIG FRAMES

Recycled items: corrugated cardboard, Christmas cards, straight twigs, ribbon, and artificial greenery

You will also need craft knife, cutting mat, craft glue, garden clippers, hot glue gun, gold spray paint, and wooden star cutouts in assorted sizes.

Allow glue and paint to dry after each application. Use hot glue for all gluing unless otherwise indicated.

SQUARE TWIG FRAME

1. Use craft knife to cut a 6" square piece of cardboard and a 3" square motif from card. Use craft glue to center and glue motif to cardboard.
2. Use garden clippers to cut twigs into $1^{3}/4$" lengths. Glue twigs around motif.
3. Paint stars gold. Tie scrap of ribbon into a bow. Glue stars, bow and greenery to frame front as desired.
4. For frame stand, bend one end of a 2" x $5^{1}/2$" cardboard piece $1^{1}/2$" to right side. With bottom of stand extending $^{1}/2$" below frame, glue area of stand above bend to back of frame. Cut a 4" length of ribbon. Gluing ribbon ends at center of bottom edges, glue ribbon to frame back and wrong side of stand.

HOUSE FRAME

1. Cut a 4" x 6" motif from card. Use craft knife to cut cardboard shape for backing (Fig. 1).

Fig. 1

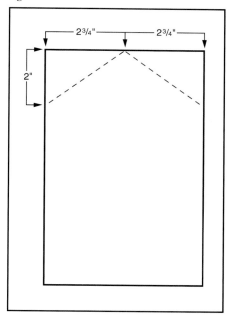

2. Center motif on cardboard 1" from bottom edge. Use craft glue to glue in place.
3. Using garden clippers and trimming to fit, glue twigs along top, bottom, then side edges of cardboard.
4. Follow Steps 3 and 4 of Square Frame to complete frame.

COMPACT CUTIE

Give an old compact new life as a pretty picture frame! This photo keeper does double duty — as a frame that displays a cherished image of a loved one and as a mirror. Scraps of wrapping paper and gold trim transform the cosmetic case into an eye-catching accent.

COMPACT FRAME

Recycled items: cosmetic compact with mirror, wrapping paper with small motifs, and gold trim

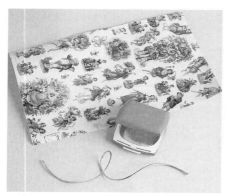

You will also need tracing paper, photograph, foam brush, craft glue, masking tape, clear acrylic spray sealer, hot glue gun, gold charms, and four ¹/₂" dia. gold beads.

Use craft glue for all gluing unless otherwise indicated. Allow sealer to dry after each application.

1. Open compact and remove cosmetic tray.
2. For photograph pattern, draw around tray on tracing paper; cut out just outside drawn lines. Centering image under pattern, draw around pattern on

photograph; cut out.
3. Mix one part glue with one part water. Cut desired motifs from wrapping paper. Use foam brush to apply glue mixture to wrong side of motifs. Overlapping as desired, glue motifs to all sides of compact without covering mirror; allow to dry.

4. Using tape to cover mirror, apply two to three coats of sealer to compact. Remove tape.
5. Glue photograph in cosmetic tray space inside compact.
6. Hot glue trim and charms to compact as desired. Hot glue beads to bottom of compact.

"CANNED" CANDLE

Oh, what fun it is to brighten a quiet corner with an attractive Yuletide accent! "Recycled" crayons are used to tint wax for the homemade candle, which is embellished with a Christmas card cutout and seasonal odds and ends.

CAN CANDLE

Recycled items: can, crayon pieces to color wax (optional), two different widths of ribbon, Christmas card, artificial greenery, small pinecones, and berries

You will also need paraffin, wax-coated wick, spray primer, red spray paint, and a hot glue gun.

Allow primer and paint to dry after each application.

1. Follow *Melting Wax,* page 157, and *Setting Wicks* page 158, to make candle in can; allow to harden.
2. Turn candle upside down. Apply one coat of primer, then two coats of paint to can.
3. Measure around can; add ¹/₂". Cut one length of each ribbon the determined

measurement. Overlapping ends, glue widest, then remaining ribbon around can.

4. Cut desired motif from Christmas card. Glue to can, covering ribbon ends.
5. Glue greenery, pinecones, and berries along bottom of can.

HAPPY-GO-LUCKY SNOWMAN

*T*his funny snow buddy is a charming gift that will liven up holiday festivities at the home of a favorite friend! Crafted from a sponge-painted mayonnaise jar, the happy-go-lucky accent is topped with a floppy felt hat.

MAYONNAISE JAR SNOWMAN

Recycled items: 32-oz. mayonnaise jar with lid, rubber band, ribbon, artificial greenery, silk flower, and fabric

You will also need white and black acrylic paint, natural sponge, tracing paper, transfer paper, paintbrush, orange paper twist, fiberfill, 10" dia. black felt circle, and a hot glue gun.

Allow paint to dry after each application.

1. Follow *Sponge Painting*, page 157, to paint jar white.
2. Trace pattern, page 141, onto tracing paper. Use transfer paper to transfer face to jar; paint eyes and mouth black.
3. For nose, cut a 1¹/₂" length of paper twist; untwist. Roll paper short end to short end. Twist one end to form a cone shape. Glue nose to jar.
4. Glue a 4" dia. ball of fiberfill to top of

lid. Place felt circle over lid; secure with rubber band. Knot ribbon around lid, covering rubber band. Glue greenery and flower to knot.

5. For muffler, tear a 1¹/₂" x 22" piece of fabric; knot around bottom of jar.

WINTRY WRAPPER

*C*reate a clever cover for a spirited gift by putting an outdated sweater to use as a wintry bottle warmer! The snuggly wrap is quickly crafted from a sweater sleeve and scraps of fabric and greenery.

SWEATER BOTTLE BAG

Recycled items: sweater, fabric, brown paper bag, and artificial greenery

You will also need a hot glue gun, green card stock, black permanent fine-point marker, hole punch, and jute twine.

1. Measure height of bottle; add 1". Measuring from finished edge of sleeve, cut a piece from sleeve the determined length.
2. For bag, turn piece wrong side out. Gather cut edge and glue to secure; turn right side out.
3. For scarf, make clips in each short end of a 2" x 18" piece of fabric. Place bottle in bag; tie scarf around neck of bottle.
4. For tag, cut a 1¹⁄₂" x 2³⁄₄" piece from card stock and a 1¹⁄₄" x 2¹⁄₄" piece from paper bag. Use marker to write desired message on paper bag piece. Center and glue paper bag piece onto card stock. Punch a hole in one corner of tag. Glue greenery to tag as desired. Use twine to tie tag to scarf.

FOLKSY FABRIC FRAMES

*A*dd *homey charm to favorite pictures with our holiday frame-ups! A practical way to package your annual gift photos, these country casual frames are simple to make — just wrap torn-fabric strips around foam food trays and finish off with woodsy bows.*

FOAM TRAY PHOTO FRAMES

Recycled items: foam food trays and acorn caps

You will also need batting, low-temperature glue gun, craft knife, cutting mat, and fabric.

1. For each frame, cut a piece of batting same size as foam tray. Glue batting to back of tray; allow to dry. Cut desired size opening from center of foam tray.
2. Tear 1"w to 1¹/₂"w strips from fabric. Overlapping strips as necessary, wrap strips around frame; glue to secure.
3. Tear a 1¹/₂" x 3¹/₂" strip of fabric. Tie a knot in center of strip. Center and glue strip to top of frame. Glue acorn cap to knot of strip.

COUNTRY SPICE

*O*ur spicy candle is a well-seasoned holiday gift! To make the candle, mold melted wax (tinted with crayon pieces) in a ready-to-spread frosting container. A wax coating with cinnamon sticks and apples adds texture and fragrance.

FROSTING CONTAINER CANDLE

Recycled items: ready-to-spread frosting container for mold, crayon pieces to color wax, and fabric

You will also need nonstick cooking spray, apples, garden clippers, cinnamon sticks, ground cinnamon, shallow pan, aluminum foil, paraffin, wax-coated wick, small basket, dried bay leaves, and a hot glue gun.

1. Spray inside of frosting container with cooking spray.
2. Cut apples into small pieces. Use clippers to cut cinnamon sticks into small pieces. Mix apples, cinnamon stick pieces, and one teaspoon ground cinnamon in shallow pan lined with foil.
3. Follow *Melting Wax*, page 157, and *Setting Wicks* page 158, to make candle; allow to harden. Remove candle from mold.

4. Dip candle in excess melted wax. Roll in apple and cinnamon mixture until desired look is achieved.
5. Dip candle in wax to seal; allow to harden. Rub ground cinnamon on top of candle.

6. Line basket with bay leaves; place candle in basket. Tear a 3/4" x 14" strip from fabric; tie into a bow. Glue bow to basket.

CRAFTY CATCH-ALL

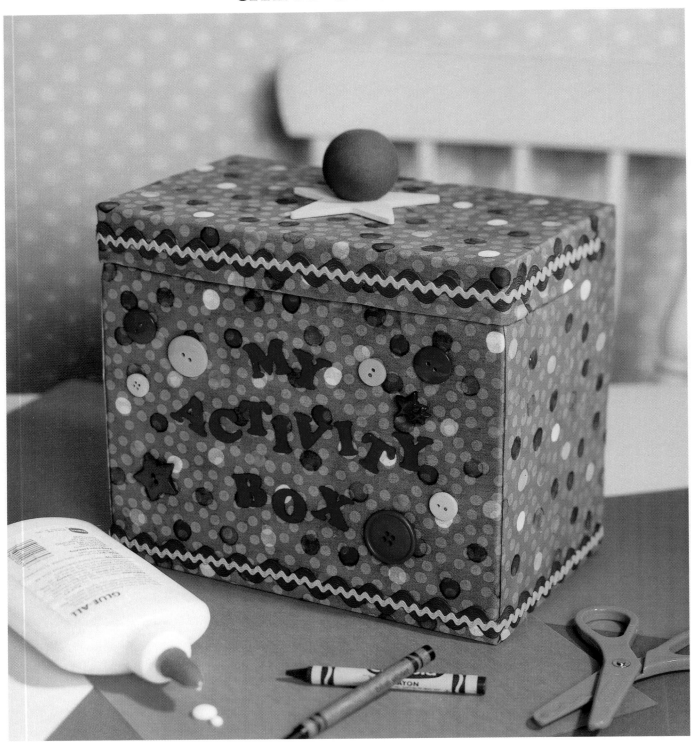

Here's a practical present for an artistic youngster — a handy holder for crafty, creative supplies. Made from a laundry detergent container, this flip-top box is a clever keeper for everything from glue to crayons and all in between!

DETERGENT BOX ART CADDY

Recycled items: large detergent box, trim and buttons

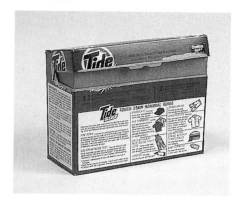

You will also need fabric, $3/4$" fusible letters, spray adhesive, hot glue gun, and a wooden star cutout and wooden knob painted to coordinate with fabric.

1. Remove handle from box.
2. Refer to Fig. 1 to measure around box from bottom edge on front of lid to top edge on front of lid; add 5". Measure lid from bottom of one side to bottom of remaining side; add 3". Cut a piece of fabric the determined measurements.

Fig. 1

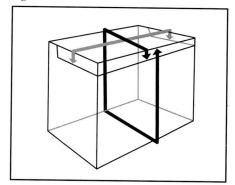

3. Apply spray adhesive to wrong side of fabric. Place box on wrong side of fabric with back bottom edge of box centered across width of wrong side of fabric. Smooth fabric around outside of box.
4. Refer to Fig. 2 to make clips in fabric where lid meets box. Pleating as necessary, smooth excess fabric to inside and ends of box. Glue fabric in place at overlaps.

Fig. 2

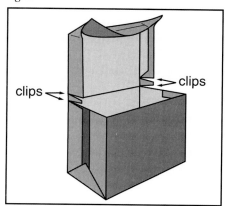

5. To cover each end of box, measure width of end of box; add 1". Measure height of end of box; add 3". Cut a piece of fabric the determined measurements. Press long edges and one short edge of fabric $1/2$" to wrong side. Apply spray adhesive to wrong side of fabric. With short pressed end at bottom of box, smooth fabric piece in place on end of box; fold excess to inside of box.
6. To line inside of lid, measure inside top of lid from front to back; add 3". Measure inside top of lid from side to side; add 1". Cut a piece of fabric the determined measurements. Press short edges and one long edge of fabric $1/2$" to wrong side. Apply spray adhesive to wrong side of fabric. With long pressed edge at front of lid and raw edge extending into box, smooth fabric in place.
7. To line bottom of box, measure length and width of bottom of box; add 1" to each measurement. Cut a piece of fabric the determined measurements. Press edges $1/2$" to wrong side. Apply spray adhesive to wrong side of fabric; smooth onto bottom of box.
8. To line inner sides of box, measure around inside of box; add 1". Measure height of inside of box; add 1". Cut a piece of fabric the determined measurements. Press long edges and one short edges $1/2$" to wrong side. Apply spray adhesive to wrong side of fabric piece. Beginning with raw edge and overlapping ends at back, smooth fabric onto inner sides of box.
9. Following manufacturer's instructions, fuse letters to fabric.
10. Center and glue trim around sides of lid and bottom of box, star and knob to top of lid, and buttons to front of box.

BRIGHT LITTLE ANGEL

*R*emind *friends and loved ones that they light up your life by presenting them with this dainty angel necklace! With a lace-scrap bodice and gold-wire halo decorating her light-bulb body, this celestial sprite is a delicate wonder.*

NIGHT LIGHT ANGEL NECKLACE

Recycled items: night light bulb, lace, and a clear plastic food container

You will also need white acrylic paint; paintbrush; 13mm wooden bead; natural sponge; hot glue gun; iridescent pearl, pink, and red dimensional paint; 1¼" of gold craft wire; ecru shredded paper; white bump chenille stem; red permanent fine-point marker; craft glue; foam brush; white tissue paper; and gold cord.

Allow paint to dry after each application. Use hot glue for all gluing unless otherwise indicated.

1. Using white acrylic paint, paint bead for head and follow *Sponge Painting*, page 157, to paint bulb for body.
2. Glue head to base of bulb; use dimensional paints to paint face.

3. For halo, form a ½" dia. circle at one end of wire. Glue remaining end into hole at top of head. Glue shredded paper to head for hair.
4. For arms, cut one bump from chenille stem; glue to center front of base of bulb. For bodice, glue lace to base of bulb, covering center of chenille stem.
5. Using marker and pattern, page 141, trace wings onto flat area of plastic container. Mix one part craft glue with one part water. Use foam brush to apply glue mixture to back of plastic over design. Place tissue paper over glue and smooth in place; allow to dry. Cut out wings. Use pearl paint to add highlights to wings. Glue wings to back of angel.
6. Glue center of a 26" length of cord to back of angel; knot ends together.

HOLIDAY TREASURE BOX

*H*ide special holiday treasures in a festive box topped with a "mosaic" Christmas card. Note cards or candy are perfect surprises to fill this container, which becomes a gift in itself!

PIECED CARD BOX

Recycled items: small box with lid, Christmas card, ribbon, and artificial greenery

You will also need red spray paint and craft glue.

Allow paint and glue to dry after each application.

1. Paint outside of box and lid red.
2. Cut desired motif from Christmas card. Cut motif into pieces. Leaving $1/16$" between pieces, arrange and glue pieces to lid.
3. Measure around sides of lid; add $1/2$". Cut a length of ribbon the determined measurement. Overlapping ends at center front, glue ribbon around sides of lid.
4. Tie a 12" length of ribbon into a bow. Covering ribbon ends, glue bow to lid. Glue greenery to knot of bow.

A favorite "shop-'til-you-drop" friend will appreciate this crafty gift! Perfect for holding shopping "necessities" and marvelous mini finds, this handy present is made by jazzing up a gallon-size plastic container with festive fabric and a cute label.

PLASTIC JUG CONTAINER

Recycled items: one-gallon plastic container and buttons

You will also need craft knife; $^1/_4$" dia. hole punch; fabrics for bucket top, letters, border, and label background; embroidery floss; small safety pin; two 1 yd. lengths of $^1/_4$"w ribbon; 2"h alphabet stencil; paper-backed fusible web; pinking shears; thick craft glue; and a black permanent fine-point marker.

1. Use craft knife to cut container to desired height. Spacing holes $^1/_2$" apart, punch an even number of holes $^1/_4$" below cut edge of container.

2. For fabric top, measure around cut edge of container; add $^1/_2$". Cut a piece of fabric $11^1/_2$" by the determined measurement. Matching right sides and using a $^1/_4$" seam allowance, sew short ends together to form a tube.

3. With seam at center back and leaving 3" between top edge and buttonhole, work a $^1/_2$" buttonhole on each side of tube for drawstring holes.

4. For casing, press top edge of tube $^1/_4$" to wrong side. Turn pressed edge $1^3/_4$" to wrong side again; press. Stitch around tube $^1/_2$" below top edge and along inner pressed edge. Turn fabric tube right side out.

5. Press raw edge of fabric tube $^1/_2$" to wrong side.

6. To attach fabric to container, place bottom edge of fabric top over container to cover holes. Using floss and beginning inside container, lace floss through one hole, fabric, button, back through button, fabric, then into next hole. Repeat to attach buttons around container (Fig. 1).

Fig. 1

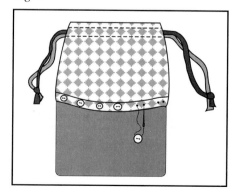

7. For drawstrings, use safety pin to thread a length of ribbon into one buttonhole, through casing, and out through same buttonhole. Repeat threading remaining length of ribbon through opposite buttonhole. Knot ribbon ends together on each side of fabric.

8. For label, use stencil to trace desired letters (in reverse) onto paper side of web. Fuse traced letters to wrong side of fabric; cut out. Remove paper backing. Arrange and fuse letters on right side of background fabric. Trim label to desired size. Center and glue label on front of container. Use pinking shears to cut four $^1/_2$"w strips from border fabric to cover edges of label; glue in place.

9. Use marker to draw "stitches" around letters.

NIFTY NECKLACE

G et into the holiday spirit by fashioning a nifty necklace of handmade paper beads for a favorite friend! Rolled beads cut from Christmas cards alternate with buttons and wooden beads on this seasonal accessory.

PAPER BEAD NECKLACE

Recycled items: Christmas cards and buttons

You will also need tracing paper, toothpick, craft glue, 32" of heavy thread, necklace clasp, and natural and red 5mm wooden beads.

1. Trace bead pattern, page 145, onto tracing paper; cut out. Draw around pattern twelve times on cards; cut out.
2. For each bead, begin at large end and roll shape around toothpick. Glue short end of bead to secure; allow to dry. Remove toothpick.
3. Tie one end of thread to clasp. String beads and buttons onto thread. Tie remaining end of thread to clasp.

102

PHOTOGRAPHIC MEMORIES

*T*o transform favorite holiday snapshots into marvelous memory-keepers, feature them on scrapbook pages trimmed with pretty Christmas cards! The cards are used as festive accents and photo "frames."

CHRISTMAS CARD MEMORY PAGES

Recycled items: Christmas cards and wrapping paper

You will also need photographs, scrapbook pages, and a glue stick.

1. Cut desired motifs and borders from cards and wrapping paper.
2. Trimming photographs to fit inside borders, arrange motifs and photographs on pages; glue in place.

This heavenly shirt is a perfect tribute for an angel of a friend. Easy appliqués and perky bias trim transform a seldom-worn shirt and scraps of fabric into this celestial topper!

APPLIQUÉD ANGEL SHIRT

Recycled items: white button-front men's shirt with front pocket, fabric scraps, and assorted buttons

You will also need tracing paper, paper-backed fusible web, two $1/4$" dia. black buttons for eyes, stencil brush, red fabric paint, red-check fabric, and red replacement buttons (optional).

1. Wash, dry, and press all fabrics.
2. Matching grey lines and arrows, trace angel body top and angel body bottom, pages 152 and 153, onto tracing paper. Using angel body pattern and patterns, pages 152 and 153, follow *Making Appliqués*, page 157, to make one each of angel body, face, mouth, hair, bow, and feet appliqués; two each of wing (one in reverse) and moon appliqués; and three star appliqués from fabric scraps. Overlapping as necessary, arrange appliqués on shirt; fuse in place. Follow *Machine Appliqué*, page 157, to stitch around appliqués.

3. Sew buttons to angel dress and stars. Sew $1/4$" dia. black buttons to face. Use stencil brush to lightly apply fabric paint to face for cheeks.
4. For trim on shirt placket, collar, pocket, and cuffs, measure along each edge to be trimmed; add 1" to each measurement. Cut a 2"w bias strip from red-check fabric for each determined measurement (pieced as necessary).
5. Press ends of bias strips $1/2$" to wrong side. Matching wrong sides and long edges, press strips in half; unfold. Matching wrong sides, press long edges to center. Refold strips.
6. Beginning at one end of edge to be trimmed and mitering corners as necessary, baste trim to right side of placket, collar, and pocket and to wrong side of each cuff. Sewing close to edges, topstitch trim in place. Fold each cuff up over sleeve.
7. If desired, replace buttons on placket.

FROSTED HOLIDAY LAMP

*B*righten a friend's day
with our jolly snowman. Crafted
using a lamp kit, this friendly
snow fellow is fashioned from a
painted jar and a self-adhesive
lampshade covered with
wintry fabric.

GLASS JAR SNOWMAN LAMP

Recycled items: fabric and a jar to fit
lamp kit

You will also need tracing paper;
transparent tape; orange, dark orange,
and black acrylic paint; paintbrushes;
clear acrylic spray sealer; gesso; jar lid
lamp kit; self-adhesive lampshade; and
fabric to cover lampshade.

*Refer to Painting Techniques, page 156,
before beginning project. Allow paint,
sealer, and gesso to dry after each
application. Gesso may take several
days to dry.*

1. Trace pattern, page 137, onto tracing
paper; cut out. Position and tape pattern
to inside of jar.
2. Paint face on outside of jar; remove
pattern. Spray jar with sealer.
3. Pour gesso into jar and swirl until

inside of jar is completely covered;
drain excess.
4. Follow manufacturer's instructions to
assemble lamp.

5. Follow manufacturer's instructions to
cover shade with fabric.
6. Tear a 1$\frac{1}{2}$" x 20" strip from fabric for
scarf; tie around jar.

SNOWY CANDLE HOLDER

Light up the holiday season with this clever candle holder. The perfect size for a votive candle, a snow-kissed flowerpot tops a mayonnaise jar embellished with tissue paper cutouts and dimensional paint "snowflakes."

CANDLE HOLDER

Recycled items: jar with 2¹/₂" dia. opening, fabric, and a votive candle

You will also need tracing paper; tape; white and black dimensional paint; yellow, green, and brown tissue paper; craft glue; paintbrush; long tweezers; and a 2¹/₂" dia. flowerpot.

Allow paint to dry after each application.

1. Trace tree and star patterns, page 137, onto tracing paper; cut out.
2. Tape patterns to inside of jar.
3. Painting on outside of jar, use black paint to outline patterns. Remove patterns.
4. Using patterns, cut yellow star, green tree, and brown trunk from tissue paper.
5. Use paintbrush to apply glue to inside of jar within painted lines of each shape. While glue is still wet, use tweezers to glue tissue shapes inside jar; allow to dry.

6. Use white paint to paint dots on outside of jar and "snow" around rim of flowerpot.

7. Tear a 1³/₄" x 17" strip of fabric; knot around neck of jar. Place flowerpot in jar. Place candle in flowerpot.

all WRAPPED up

*O*h, what fun it is to wrap a flurry of holiday presents in creative containers made from throwaway materials! Inside this section, we'll show you how to craft charming bags, boxes, and cans from snack containers, brown bags, and such. You'll even find gleaming gift wrap made from newspaper! You can deliver tasty treats in handsome containers made from checkbook boxes or cross stitch-topped canisters that once contained chips. After creatively packaging your presents in our festive gift holders, you'll be convinced that "recycled" wraps are fun and fancy ways to put finishing touches on your most special presents!

PRETTY PAPER STOCKINGS

These pretty paper stockings, made of brown bags, fabric scraps, and buttons, are perfect holders for holiday surprises! Our charming country stockings are easy to craft using decorative-edge scissors and easy appliqué techniques.

PAPER BAG STOCKINGS

BASIC STOCKING

Recycled items: large brown paper bags, fabrics, and buttons

You will also need tracing paper, decorative-edge craft scissors, paper-backed fusible web, hole punch, and jute twine.

1. Open bag at back seam. Cut bottom from bag. Flatten bag piece. For cuff, fold one long edge $1^7/8$" to unprinted side; repeat. Matching short edges and printed sides, fold bag in half.
2. Matching grey lines and arrows, trace stocking top and stocking bottom patterns, pages 150 and 151, onto tracing paper. Align top edge of pattern with folded cuff edge of bag. Follow Steps 1 and 2 of *Sewing Shapes*, page 159, to make stocking. Use craft scissors to cut out stocking $1/4$" from stitched line.
3. Using patterns, pages 150 and 151, follow *Making Appliqués*, page 157, to make cuff, heel, and toe appliqués in reverse from fabrics. Arrange and fuse appliqués to stocking.
4. For handles, punch two holes $1/2$" from top and 3" apart through all layers of stocking cuff. Cut two 16" lengths of twine. Thread ends of one twine length from inside to outside through holes in stocking front. Knot ends. Repeat for stocking back.

ANGEL STOCKING

Recycled items: fabrics, thread, and buttons
You will also need Basic Stocking, craft glue, jute twine, black permanent fine-point marker, and a 1" dia. two-hole button for head.

1. For wings, tear a $4^1/2$" square from fabric; gather at center and secure with thread. Glue wings to stocking.
2. For arms, cut an 8" length of twine; knot ends. For dress, tear a $4^1/2$" square from fabric. Gather one edge and secure with thread. Glue arms, then dress to wings.
3. For head, use holes in button for eyes and marker to draw mouth on button. For halo, cut a $1^1/2$" length of twine; glue ends to back of button. Glue head to angel.
4. Glue buttons to stocking as desired.

CHRISTMAS TREE STOCKING

Recycled items: fabrics and buttons
You will also need Basic Stocking, pinking shears, brown felt, paper-backed fusible web, jute twine, and a $1^3/4$"w star-shaped wooden cutout.

1. For branches, tear one each of the following strips from fabric: $1^1/4$" x 7", $1^1/4$" x $6^1/2$", $1^1/4$" x $6^1/4$", $1^1/4$" x 6", $1^1/4$" x $5^1/2$", 1" x 5", and 1" x $4^1/2$". Tie a knot in center of each strip.
2. For tree trunk, use pinking shears to cut a $3/4$" x 7" piece from felt. Glue trunk to stocking. Arrange and glue knots of branches to trunk.
3. Using pattern, page 150, follow *Making Appliqués*, page 157, to make star appliqué from fabric. Center and fuse appliqué to wooden cutout. Glue star to top of tree.
4. Glue buttons to stocking as desired.

WOODSY CHRISTMAS CANS

*P*acked with your extra-special edibles, our rustic holiday cans appeal to both the eye and the taste buds! It's super simple to fuse adorable fabric-scrap appliqués to snowy white fabric, then wrap it around "recycled" canisters.

FABRIC-COVERED CANS

Recycled items: cans with lids, assorted fabrics, and ribbon

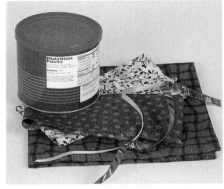

You will also need paper-backed fusible web, spray adhesive, craft glue, and raffia.

1. For each can, remove lid. Measure height of can between rims. Measure around can; add $1/2$". Cut a piece of fabric the determined measurements for background.
2. Using patterns, page 144, follow *Making Appliqués*, page 157, to make desired appliqués from fabrics. Arrange and fuse appliqués to background.
3. Apply spray adhesive to wrong side of background. Overlapping ends at back, smooth fabric around can.

4. Overlapping ends at back and trimming to fit, glue ribbon along bottom edge of can.

5. Place gift in can; replace lid. Tie several lengths of raffia into a bow around can.

REINDEER FEED BAG

*O*ur *favorite reindeer's bright red nose blazes the way on this charming gift bag. Designed to hold yummy holiday treats, the goodie holder is fashioned from a brown paper bag embellished with twigs and a bottle cap.*

BROWN PAPER REINDEER BAG

Recycled items: poster board, metal bottle cap, artificial greenery, and twigs

You will also need tracing paper, black permanent fine-point marker, spray primer, white and red spray paint, hot glue gun, lunch-size brown paper bag, and jute twine.

Allow primer and paint to dry after each application.

1. Trace pattern, page 144, onto tracing paper; cut out. Draw around pattern two times on poster board. Use marker to color eyes; cut out.
2. For nose, spray bottle cap with primer, then red paint. Glue eyes and nose to one side of bag. Use marker to draw mouth.

3. Place gift in bag. Gather top of bag; knot twine around gathers to secure. Glue greenery to twine.

4. For antlers, paint twigs white. Glue antlers to back of reindeer under twine.

Enchant the folks on your gift list with crafty containers featuring homespun holiday motifs. We wrapped empty food cans with festive fabrics and added fun figures cut from aluminum beverage cans.

SODA CAN CUTOUT TINS

Recycled items: assorted-size food cans, red aluminum beverage cans, and a push pin

For each can, you will also need white spray primer, brown spray paint, fabric, spray adhesive, hammer, nail, medium-gauge craft wire, tracing paper, black permanent fine-point marker, and gold fine-gauge craft wire.
For star garland can, you will also need wooden beads.
For angel can, you will also need a hole punch and household cement.

STAR GARLAND CAN

1. Allowing to dry between each coat, spray food can with primer, then brown paint.
2. Measure around food can; add ¹/₂". Measure height of can between rims. Cut a piece from fabric the determined measurements. Apply spray adhesive to wrong side of fabric; smooth fabric around can, overlapping at back.
3. Use hammer and nail to punch a hole in each side of food can. For handle, insert ends of desired length of medium-gauge wire into holes; twist to secure.
4. Cut through opening and down to bottom of two beverage cans; cut away top and bottom of cans. Flatten can pieces.
5. Using spray adhesive, glue right sides of can pieces together.
6. Trace star pattern, page 146, onto tracing paper; cut out. Use marker to draw around pattern desired number of times on beverage can pieces. Cut out stars.
7. Use push pin to punch holes along edges of each star. Lace fine-gauge wire through holes along edges of each star.
8. Thread stars and beads onto a length of fine-gauge wire. Twist ends of wire around each side of handle.

ANGEL CAN

1. Follow Steps 1 - 3 of Star Garland Can to prepare food can.
2. Cut through opening and down to bottom of three beverage cans; cut away top and bottom of cans. Flatten can pieces.
3. Using spray adhesive, glue right sides of two can pieces together.
4. Trace angel and wings patterns, page 146, onto tracing paper; cut out.

Use marker to draw around angel on glued can pieces and around wings on remaining can piece; cut out shapes. For buttons, use hole punch to punch dots from remaining portion of single layer can piece.
5. Use push pin to punch holes at random in wings and along edges of angel. Lace fine-gauge wire through holes along edges of angel. For hair, cut an 8" length of fine-gauge wire. Leaving ¹/₂" loops of wire between holes, lace wire through holes along edge of head. Twist loops to shape hair.
6. Use household cement to glue wings to back of angel and wrong side of buttons to front of angel. Thread a length of fine-gauge wire through one hole in each side of neck. Twist ends of wire around each side of handle.

GINGERBREAD MAN CAN

1. Follow Steps 1 - 3 of Star Garland Can to prepare food can.
2. Follow Steps 2 and 3 of Angel Can to prepare beverage cans.
3. Trace gingerbread man and heart patterns, page 146, onto tracing paper; cut out. Use marker to draw around gingerbread man on glued can pieces and around heart three times on remaining can piece; cut out shapes.
4. Use push pin to punch holes along edges of gingerbread man, two holes for eyes, and two holes in each heart. Lace fine-gauge wire through holes along edges of gingerbread man.
5. Thread hearts onto a length of fine-gauge wire. Twist ends of wire around ends of gingerbread man arms. Thread a length of fine-gauge wire through one hole in each arm. Twist ends of wire around each side of handle.

"CHECK" IT OUT

L et friends "check" out how delicious treats look when displayed in our handsome holiday gift boxes! Featuring cellophane "windows," simple checkbook boxes are embellished with wrapping paper, ribbon scraps, and gold paint.

CHECK BOX GIFT CONTAINERS

Recycled items: checkbook boxes, wrapping paper, ribbon, and artificial greenery

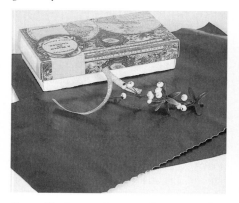

You will also need spray adhesive, craft glue, craft knife, cutting mat, clear cellophane, gold dimensional paint, gold acrylic paint, paintbrush, and a hot glue gun.

1. For each container, remove lid from box. Measure length and width of lid including each side (Fig. 1). Add 1" to each measurement. Cut a piece of paper the determined measurements. Apply spray adhesive to wrong side of paper. Center lid top side down on wrong side of paper piece. Folding paper to inside of lid and pleating corners as necessary, smooth edges of paper piece to inside of lid.

Fig. 1

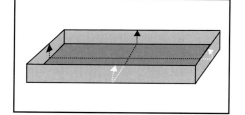

2. Draw a 2" x 3" rectangle at center of lid. Use craft knife to carefully cut out opening along drawn lines.

3. Cut a 3" x 4" piece of cellophane. Use craft glue to glue cellophane over opening on inside of lid. Cover edges of opening with a line of dimensional paint; allow to dry.
4. Place gift in box. Measure around box; add 6". Cut a length of ribbon the determined measurement. Knot ribbon around box. Tie a 10" length of ribbon into a bow.
5. Use acrylic paint to add highlights to greenery. Glue greenery and bow to knot of ribbon on lid.

GLEAMING GIFT WRAP

*G*leaming with the grandeur
of King Midas' gold, our holiday
wrap adds mystery and magic to
your holiday gifts. You can create
this metallic look by coating
ordinary newspaper with bronze
and gold spray paints. The silvery
marbling is produced with paint-
dipped string.

NEWSPAPER GIFT WRAP

Recycled items: newspaper, magnolia
leaves, and pinecones

You will also need gold and bronze spray
paint, string, silver acrylic paint,
paintbrush, and a hot glue gun.

*Allow paint to dry after each
application.*

1. Spray newspaper with gold, then
bronze paint.
2. Dip a length of string in silver paint;
place string on paper and press lightly.
Repeat for each design.
3. For gift decorations, spray leaves and
pinecones with gold or bronze paint.
Highlight tips of pinecones with silver
paint. Glue leaves and pinecones to
wrapped gifts.

HANDSOME GIFT BAGS

*M*ake *your holiday gift-giving merry and bright by packaging presents in one-of-a-kind gift bags! To craft the handsome holders, cut apart Christmas cards from bygone years, piece them together on colorful card stock, and glue to the bags along with scrap-ribbon bows.*

PIECED CARD GIFT BAGS

Recycled items: Christmas cards and ribbon

Use craft glue for all gluing unless otherwise indicated. Allow glue to dry after each application.

BAG WITH HANDLE

You will also need craft glue, red and green card stock, gift bag with handle, artificial greenery, and a hot glue gun.

1. Cut desired motif from card; cut into pieces. Leaving ¹/₁₆" between pieces, arrange and glue pieces to red card stock.
2. Leaving a ¹/₁₆" red border, cut out design. Center and glue design to green card stock. Leaving a ¹/₈" green border, cut out design. Center and glue green card stock to a second piece of red card stock. Leaving a ¹/₄" red border, cut out design. Glue design to front of bag.
3. Tie a 26" length of ribbon into a bow. Hot glue bow and greenery to front of bag.

FOLDED BAG

You will also need tracing paper, red card stock, craft glue, and a bag at least 8"w.

1. Trace pattern, page 154, onto tracing paper; cut out. Using pattern, cut oval from card stock.
2. Cut desired motif from card; cut into pieces. Leaving ¹/₁₆" between pieces, arrange and glue pieces to oval.
3. Insert gift in bag and fold top of bag 3" to front. Center and glue oval over flap of bag.
4. Tie a 16" length of ribbon into a bow; glue to bag.

GLITTERING GIFTS

*T*o double the pleasure of
*your holiday gift-giving, wrap
your presents in our fun, festive
gift holders. Gilded produce
containers and ordinary white
gift boxes become glittering
wonders when embellished
with Yuletide napkin motifs.*

GIFT BOXES

Recycled items: white gift boxes, produce
containers, and artificial greenery (optional)

You will also need gold acrylic paint,
natural sponge, decorative napkins, spray
adhesive, assorted ribbons and cord, hot
glue gun, 2" dia. jingle bell, and gold
spray paint.

Allow paint to dry after each application.

GIFT BOXES
1. For each box, follow *Sponge Painting*,
page 157, and use acrylic paint to paint
box if desired.
2. Separate plies of napkins. Cut desired
motifs from napkins. Apply spray adhesive
to wrong side of motifs. Position and
smooth motifs onto lid.
3. Place gift in box. Tie ribbons and cord
into bows around box as desired. Glue
greenery or bell to bow.

PRODUCE CONTAINER BOXES
1. For each box, spray paint produce
container gold.

2. Follow Steps 2 and 3 of Gift Boxes to
finish boxes.

ELFIN ORGANIZER

*A*n expert at wrapping toys for good little girls and boys, our super-organized elf helps you find a niche for all your gift wrapping necessities. Fashioned from a sponge-painted detergent box, this convenient gift wrap caddy features handy compartments made from fabric-covered checkbook boxes.

DETERGENT BOX WRAPPING CENTER

Recycled items: large detergent box, poster board, cardboard, two checkbook boxes, ribbon, and two buttons

You will also need craft knife; cutting mat; masking tape; red spray paint; white, flesh, and black acrylic paint; natural sponge; clear acrylic matte spray sealer; fabric; spray adhesive; tracing paper; transfer paper; black permanent fine-point marker; gesso; paintbrush; hot glue gun; medium-gauge craft wire; wire cutters; and wooden beads.

Refer to Painting Techniques, page 156, before beginning project. Allow paint, sealer, and gesso to dry after each application.

1. Cut lid from detergent box. Cut a $1/2$" dia. hole at center in each end of box 1" below top edge.
2. Cover top edge of detergent box with masking tape. Spray paint box red. Sponge paint box white. Spray box with sealer.
3. Cut one 8" x 10" piece each from poster board and fabric. Apply spray adhesive to wrong side of fabric and smooth onto poster board.
4. Trace patterns, page 154, onto tracing paper. Use transfer paper to transfer two mittens (one in reverse) and head onto fabric-covered poster board. Use marker to draw over transferred lines.
5. Apply gesso to face and fur trim areas; paint face. Use marker to add details to face, hat, and mittens; cut out. Spray with sealer. Glue head and mittens to box.
6. Determine desired length of handle; add 2". Cut a length of wire the determined measurement. Insert one end of wire through hole in one end of box; glue 1" to inside of box to secure. Thread beads onto wire. Insert remaining end of wire into hole on opposite end of box; glue 1" to inside of box to secure.
7. For section dividers inside box, measure width and length of box; subtract $1/8$" from each measurement. Measure height of box at front of box; subtract $1/4$".

For short divider, cut one piece from cardboard the determined width and height measurements. For long divider, cut one piece from cardboard the determined length and height measurements.
8. Mark across short divider from top to bottom at center. Mark across long divider from top to bottom at desired placement of section division. Leaving 1" uncut, cut across each divider where marked. Paint dividers red.
9. Place long divider cut side up in center of box. Place short divider cut side down over cut in long divider; glue to secure.
10. Glue checkbook boxes closed. Cut 2" from one end of one box. Cut second box in half.
11. For each box, measure around box; add $1/2$". Measure height of box; add 3". Cut a piece of fabric the determined measurement. Apply spray adhesive to wrong side of fabric. Centering box on fabric and overlapping ends at back, smooth fabric around box. Fold excess fabric to inside of box and across bottom of box, clipping corners as necessary.
12. Cut three 1" x $2^1/2$" labels from poster board. Use marker to write "Tags," "Scissors," and "Tape" on labels. Glue labels to boxes. Glue boxes to front of organizer.
13. Tie two 15" lengths of ribbon into bows. Glue bows to front of organizer. Glue buttons to bows.

CHARMING GOODIE PAILS

Charm your friends by filling darling wire-handled cans with their favorite treats. The quick-to-fix cans are spray-painted, then decorated with buttons, bows, and felt.

FOOD CAN GIFT CONTAINERS

Recycled items: cans, fabric, buttons, felt, and poster board

You will also need grey spray primer, red spray paint, hammer, nail, wire cutters, black craft wire, decorative-edge craft scissors, and a hot glue gun.

Allow primer and paint to dry after each application.

BOW CONTAINER
1. Turn can upside down. Spray outside of can with primer, then paint. Use hammer and nail to punch a hole on each side of can.
2. For handle, insert one end of a 14" length of wire through one hole; twist to secure. Shape loops in wire as desired. Insert opposite end through hole in opposite side of can; twist to secure.
3. Measure around can; add 14". Tear a strip of fabric 1¹/₂"w by the determined measurement; tie into a bow around can.

BUTTON CONTAINER
1. Follow Step 1 of Bow Container to prepare can.
2. For handle, insert one end of an 18" length of wire through one hole; twist to secure. Threading buttons onto wire at each loop, shape loops in wire as desired. Insert opposite end through hole in opposite side of can; twist to secure.
3. Measure around can; add ¹/₂". Use craft scissors to cut a piece of felt 2¹/₄"w by the determined measurement. Overlapping ends at back, glue felt around can.
4. Add 4" to measurement determined in Step 3. Tear a strip of fabric 1¹/₄"w by the determined measurement. Knot strip around can; glue button to knot.

STAR CONTAINER
For star container, you will also need star-shaped wooden cutouts, spray adhesive, and embroidery floss.

1. Follow Step 1 of Bow Container to prepare can. Paint wooden cutouts red.
2. For handle, thread ends of a 9" length of wire through holes in can; twist ends to secure.
3. Measure around can; add ¹/₂". Cut a piece of fabric 3"w by the determined measurement, a piece of poster board 2¹/₂"w by the determined measurement, and a piece of felt 1³/₄"w by the determined measurement.
4. Apply spray adhesive to wrong side of fabric. Center poster board on fabric. Fold fabric edges to back of poster board. Overlapping ends at back, glue fabric-covered poster board around can.
5. Using floss, work *Blanket Stitch,* page 158, along long edges of felt piece. Overlapping ends at back, center and glue felt over fabric-covered poster board.
6. Glue stars to can and buttons to stars.

ONE-OF-A-KIND GIFT BAGS

Have a ball creating one-of-a-kind gift bags using cutouts from Christmas cards received in past years! Highlighted with fabric and Yuletide accents, these totes will be a hit with folks on your gift list.

CARD-EMBELLISHED BAGS

LARGE WHITE GIFT BAG
Recycled items: Christmas card, fabric, and artificial holly with berries
You will also need tracing paper, craft glue, 8" x 10" white gift bag, card stock, decorative-edge craft scissors, and 1¹/₂"w wired ribbon.

1. Cut desired motif from card. Trace areas of motif to be covered with fabric onto tracing paper; cut out. Using patterns, cut shapes from fabric; glue to motif. Glue motif to bag.
2. Glue a sprig of holly to motif.
3. For label, cut desired message from card; glue to card stock. Using craft scissors and leaving a ¹/₄" border, cut out label; glue to bag.
4. Tie a 28" length of ribbon into a bow; glue to front of bag.

SMALL WHITE GIFT BAG
Recycled items: fabric, Christmas card, artificial miniature holly garland, and gold cord
You will also need 5" x 8" white gift bag, spray adhesive, craft glue, three colors of ¹/₈"w satin ribbon, ³/₄" dia. jingle bell, permanent fine-point marker, card stock, decorative-edge craft scissors, and a hole punch.

1. Cut a piece of fabric slightly smaller than front of bag. Apply spray adhesive to wrong side of fabric; smooth onto front of bag.
2. Cut desired motif from card; glue to front of bag. Trimming to fit, glue garland around motif.
3. Thread ribbons through shank of bell; tie ribbons together into a bow. Glue bow to bag.

4. For tag, cut desired message from card. Use marker to draw "stitches" along edge of tag; glue to card stock. Using craft scissors and leaving a ¹/₄" border, cut out tag. Punch hole in tag. Use a 6" length of cord to tie tag to bag.

BROWN PAPER GIFT BAG
Recycled items: Christmas card (we used a card with a bear motif), fabric, ribbon, and gold cord
You will also need craft glue, tracing paper, lunch-size brown paper bag, items to decorate card (we used black cabochons for eyes and a toothpick and white acrylic paint to add highlights to eyes), hole punch, card stock, and decorative-edge craft scissors.

1. Cut desired motif from card. Trace areas of motif to be covered with fabric onto tracing paper; cut out. Using patterns, cut shapes from fabric; glue to motif. If desired, glue decorative items to motif. Glue motif to bag.
2. Place gift in bag. Fold top of bag 1³/₄" to back. Punch two holes 1¹/₂" apart at center top of bag. Thread a 12" length of ribbon through holes and tie into a bow at front of bag.
3. For tag, cut desired message from card; glue to card stock. Using craft scissors and leaving a ¹/₄" border, cut out tag. Punch hole in tag. Use a 6" length of cord to tie tag to bag.

SNOW BUDDIES

*O*ur bird-in-hand snowman is a bright and cheery way to package holiday treats! Accented with textured snow paint, a snack chip container becomes a rustic-looking snow fellow.

CHIP CAN SNOWMAN

Recycled items: snack chip container, red adult-size sock, fabric scraps, twigs, and three black buttons

You will also need white spray primer, white spray paint, stencil brush, textured snow paint, fiberfill, hot glue gun, nail, wire cutters, two $1/4$" dia. black shank buttons, craft stick, orange acrylic paint, paintbrush, and a $1^1/2$" red wooden bird.

Allow primer and paints to dry after each application.

1. For snowman, spray container with two coats each of primer, then white paint. Using stencil brush, apply snow paint to container.
2. For hat, fold cuff of sock up 1"; repeat. For tassel, cut a 1" x 4" piece of fabric; roll short end to short end. Tack one end to toe of sock and make clips in opposite end.

3. Glue a 3" dia. ball of fiberfill to top of lid. Arrange and glue hat on snowman.
4. For arms, use nail to make one pilot hole in each side of snowman; insert twigs in holes.
5. For eyes, use wire cutters to remove shanks from buttons. For nose, paint one end of craft stick orange; cut $3/4$" from painted end of stick. Glue eyes, nose, and buttons to snowman.
6. For scarf, tear a 1" x 18" strip of fabric. Knot scarf around snowman. Glue bird to arm.

CHRISTMAS JOY

*F*or homemade gifts from the heart, cross stitch a trio of holiday toppers for Yuletide containers! Make each holder an individual delight by using a variety of festive wrapping papers and ribbon scraps.

CROSS STITCH CANISTERS

Recycled items: snack chip containers with lid, wrapping paper, and ribbon

You will also need embroidery floss (see color key, page 155), 6" square of 14 count white Aida, tracing paper, craft glue, spray adhesive, and curling ribbon.

Refer to Cross Stitch (page 159), before beginning project.

1. For each canister, use two strands of floss for Cross Stitch and one strand of floss for Backstitch to work desired design, page 155, on Aida.
2. Trace around lid on tracing paper; cut out. Use pattern to cut out design. Glue design to top of lid; allow to dry.
3. Measure height of container. Measure around container; add ¹/₂". Cut a piece of wrapping paper the determined measurements. Apply spray adhesive to wrong side of paper. Overlapping ends at

back, smooth paper around container. Glue a length of ribbon around bottom of container; allow to dry.

4. Tie curling ribbon around container; curl ends.

PATTERNS

PAPER TUBE NUTCRACKER
(Page 9)

Face

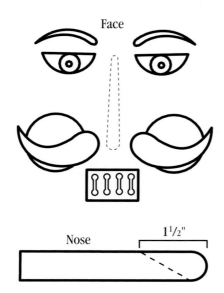

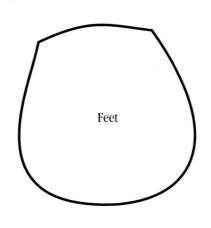

Feet

Nose   1$^{1}/_{2}$"

FOAM TRAY SNOWFLAKES
(Page 54)

NEWSPAPER NOSEGAY
(Page 10)

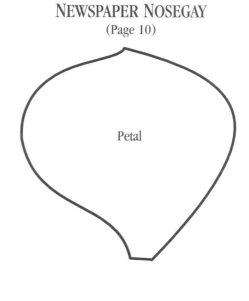

Petal

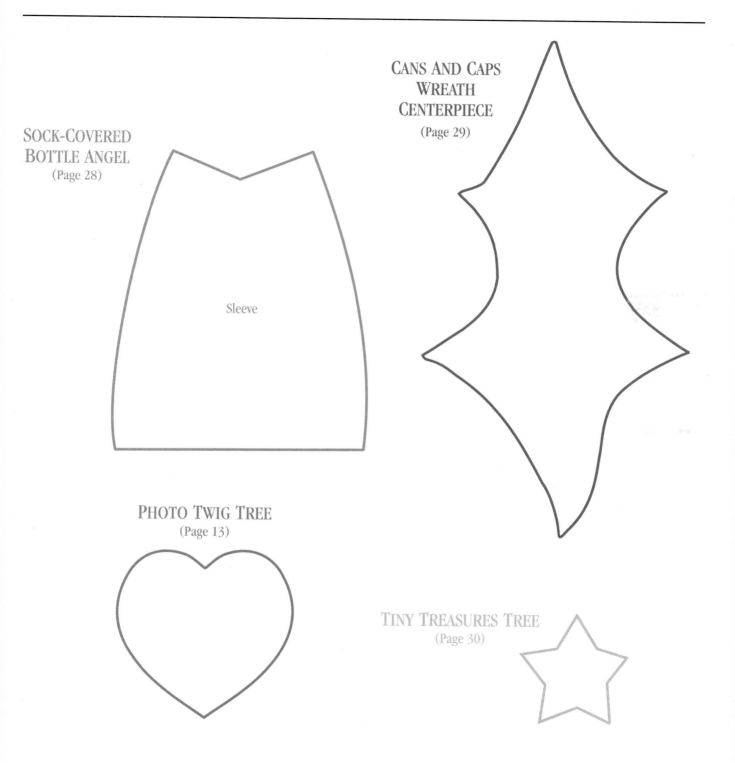

SOCK-COVERED
BOTTLE ANGEL
(Page 28)

Sleeve

CANS AND CAPS
WREATH
CENTERPIECE
(Page 29)

PHOTO TWIG TREE
(Page 13)

TINY TREASURES TREE
(Page 30)

PATTERNS (continued)

PAPER CARTON BIRDHOUSES
(Pages 15 and 16)

Design A

Design D

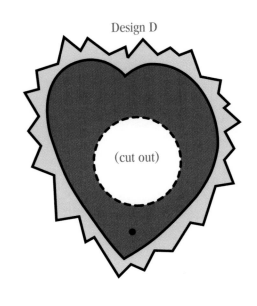

Design B

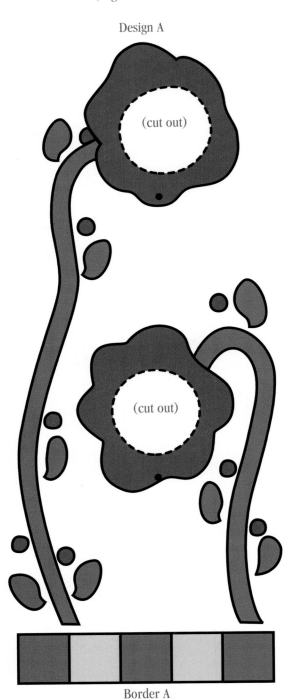

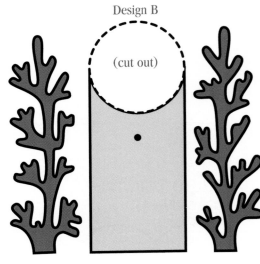

Border A

Border B

Design C

(cut out)

Border C

VINYL FLOORING SNOWMAN
(Page 45)

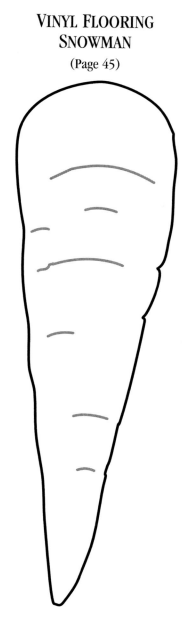

PATTERNS (continued)

FOOD CONTAINER
"LIGHT" STRAND
(Page 67)

Bulb

Plug

Socket

NATURALS
GARLAND
(Page 22)

SODA BOTTLE
SNOWMAN
(Page 46)

Nose

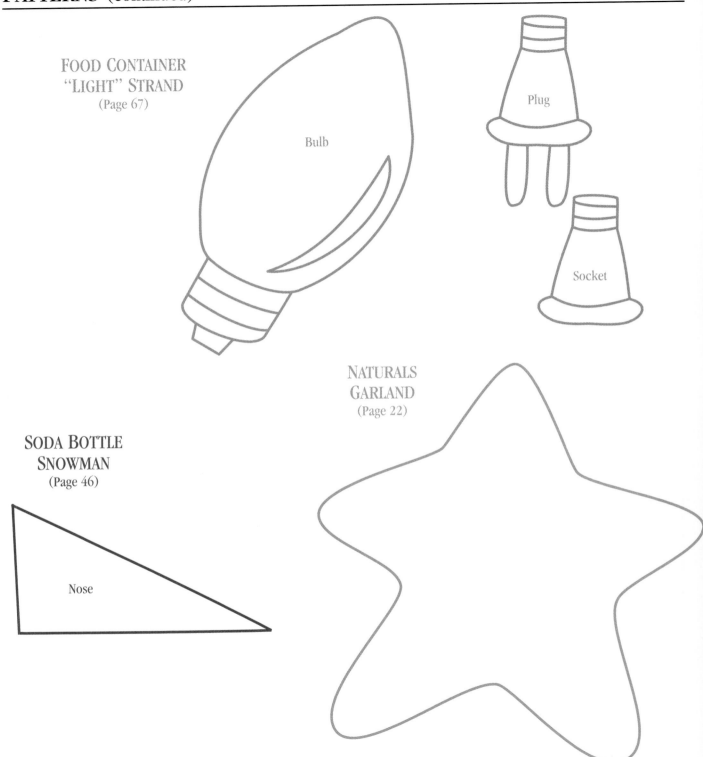

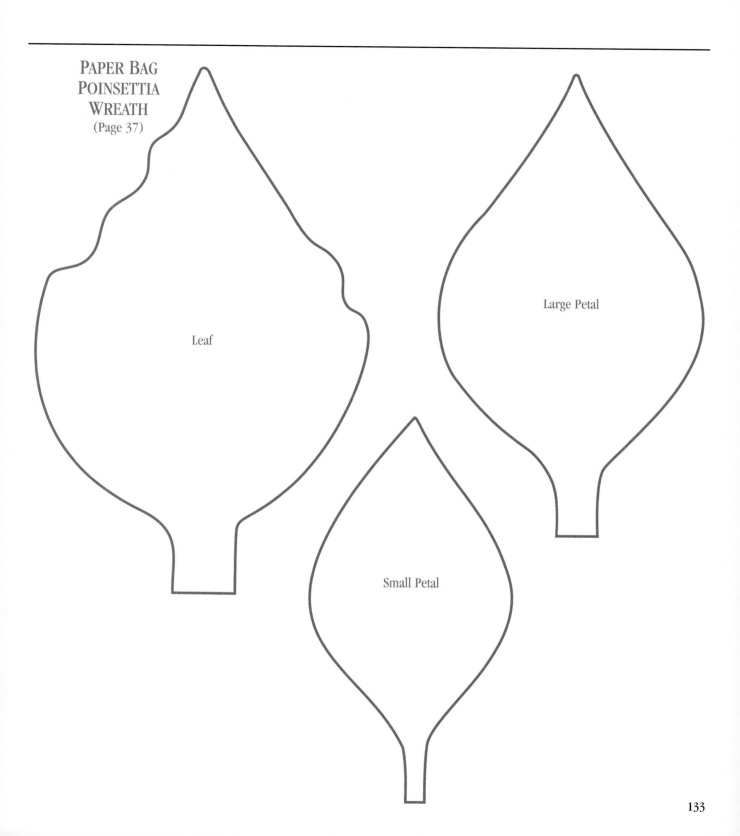

PAPER BAG
POINSETTIA
WREATH
(Page 37)

Leaf

Large Petal

Small Petal

133

PATTERNS (continued)

JUICE LID
SNOW PALS
(Page 81)

CREW SOCK
STOCKINGS
(Page 38)

PRODUCE CONTAINER SANTA
(Page 43)

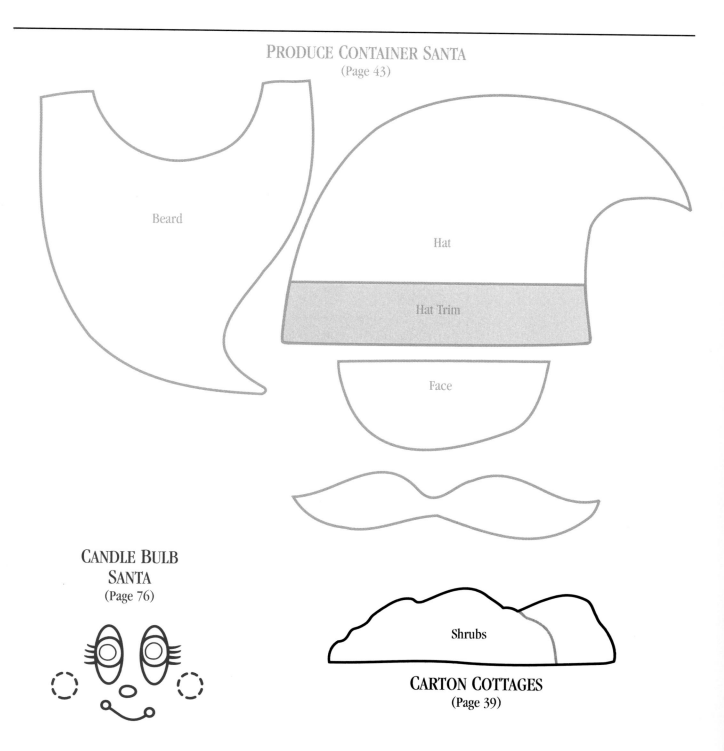

Beard

Hat

Hat Trim

Face

CANDLE BULB
SANTA
(Page 76)

Shrubs

CARTON COTTAGES
(Page 39)

FABRIC BOLT
SNOWMEN
(Page 40)

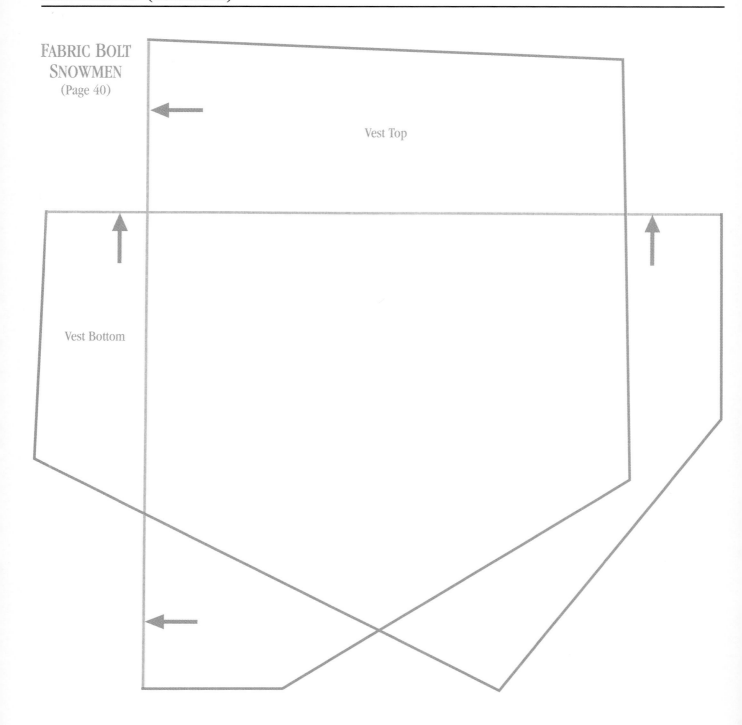

Vest Top

Vest Bottom

136

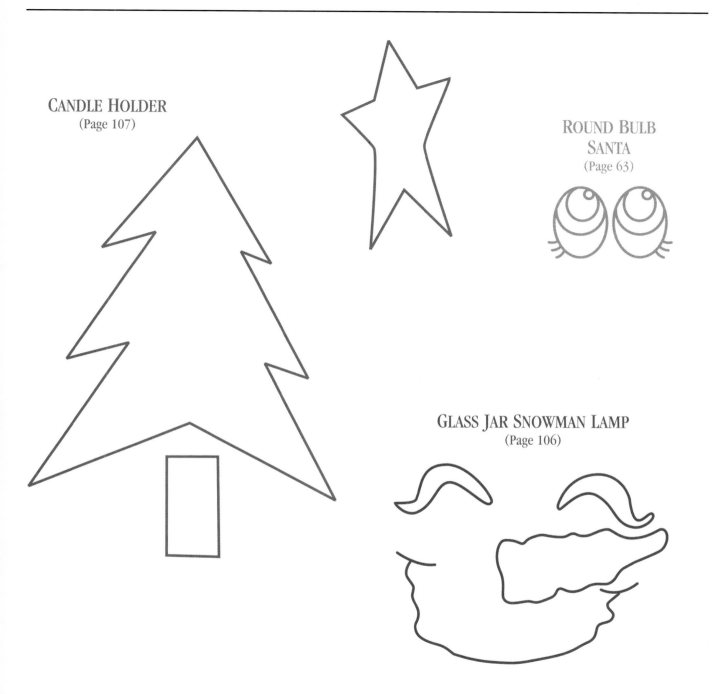

CANDLE HOLDER
(Page 107)

ROUND BULB
SANTA
(Page 63)

GLASS JAR SNOWMAN LAMP
(Page 106)

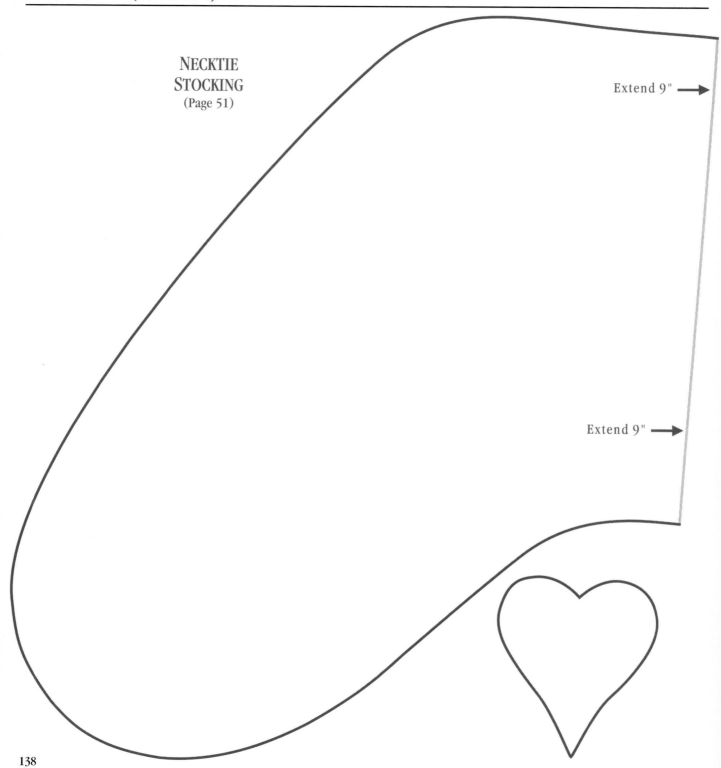

NECKTIE
STOCKING
(Page 51)

Extend 9" ⟶

Extend 9" ⟶

NECKTIE STAR
ORNAMENT
(Page 55)

PATTERNS (continued)

FOAM TRAY
DOVE
(Page 64)

WING

DOVE

PLASTIC LID STAR
GARLAND
(Page 65)

MAYONNAISE JAR
SNOWMAN
(Page 92)

MINI CAN
SANTA CUPS
(Page 68)

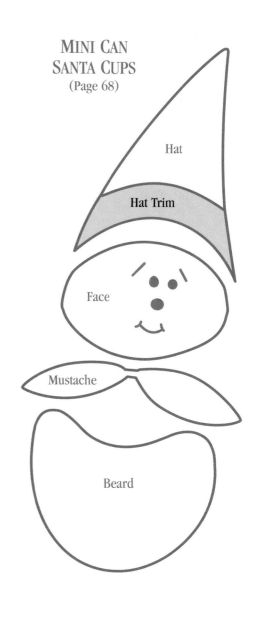

Hat

Hat Trim

Face

Mustache

Beard

NIGHT LIGHT
ANGEL NECKLACE
(Page 98)

PATTERNS (continued)

SWEATER STOCKING
(Page 19)

FLANNEL SHIRT STOCKING
(Page 27)

Stocking Top

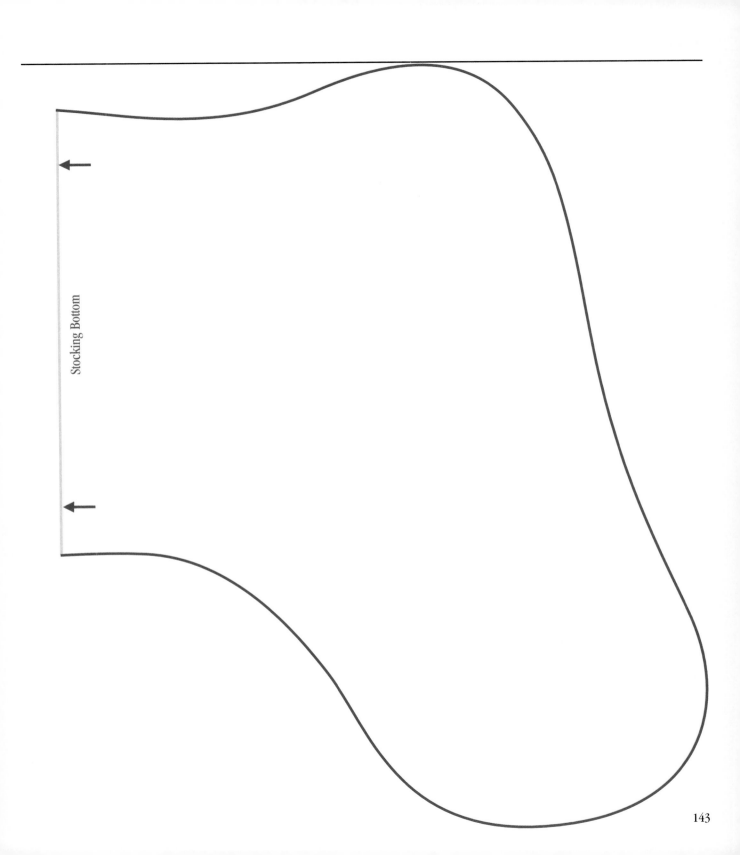

Stocking Bottom

PATTERNS (continued)

BEARDED SANTA CANS
(Page 79)

PAPER BAG
REINDEER TEAM
(Page 47)

BROWN PAPER
REINDEER BAG
(Page 113)

FABRIC-COVERED CANS
(Page 112)

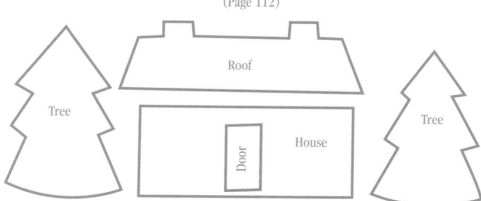

Roof

Tree

Door

House

Tree

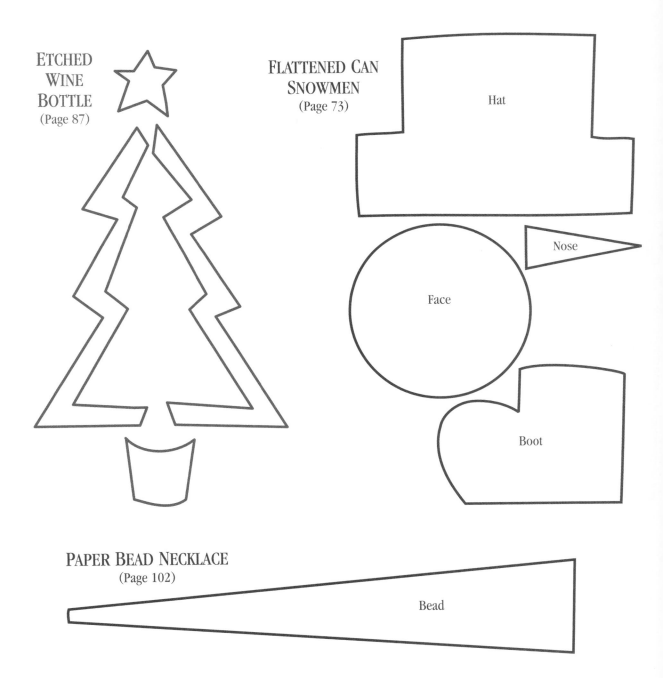

ETCHED
WINE
BOTTLE
(Page 87)

FLATTENED CAN
SNOWMEN
(Page 73)

Hat

Nose

Face

Boot

PAPER BEAD NECKLACE
(Page 102)

Bead

SODA CAN CUTOUT TINS
(Page 115)

**PAPER BAG
SNOWMAN**
(Page 56)

FOOD CONTAINER
SANTA ORNAMENTS
(Page 77)

PATTERNS (continued)

PAPER BAG STOCKINGS
(page 111)

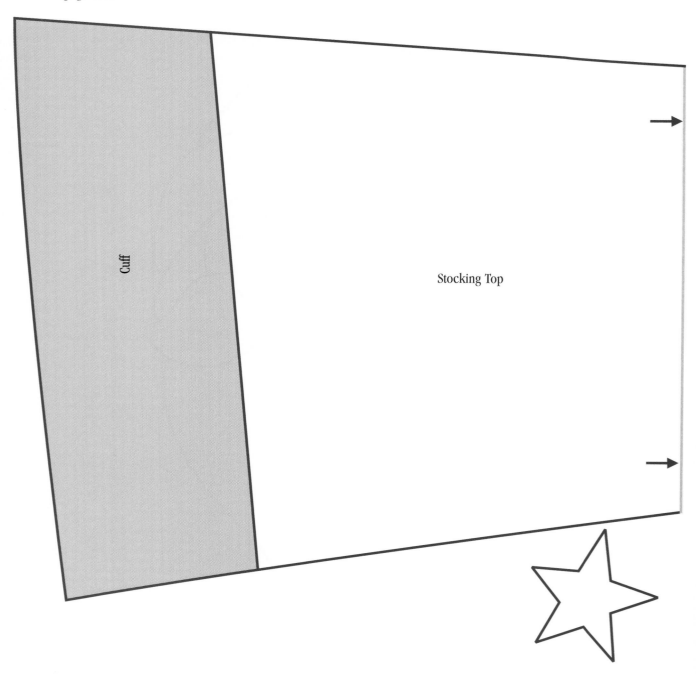

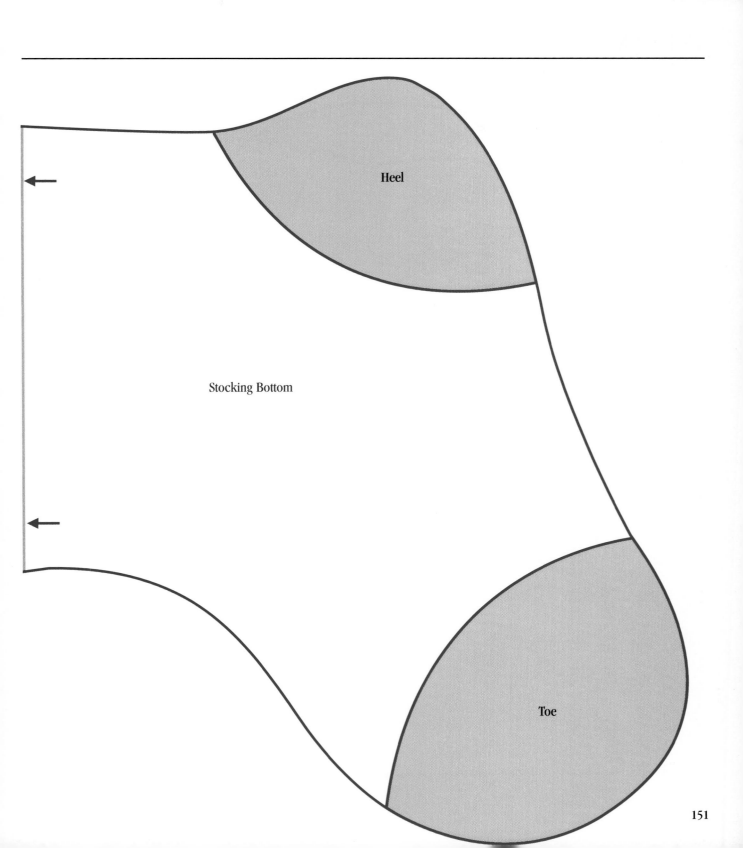

Heel

Stocking Bottom

Toe

PATTERNS (continued)

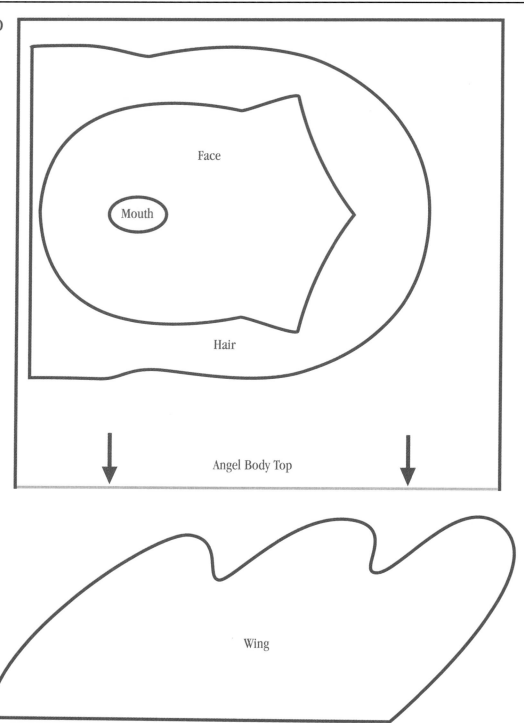

APPLIQUÉD
ANGEL
SHIRT
(Page 105)

Face

Mouth

Hair

Angel Body Top

Wing

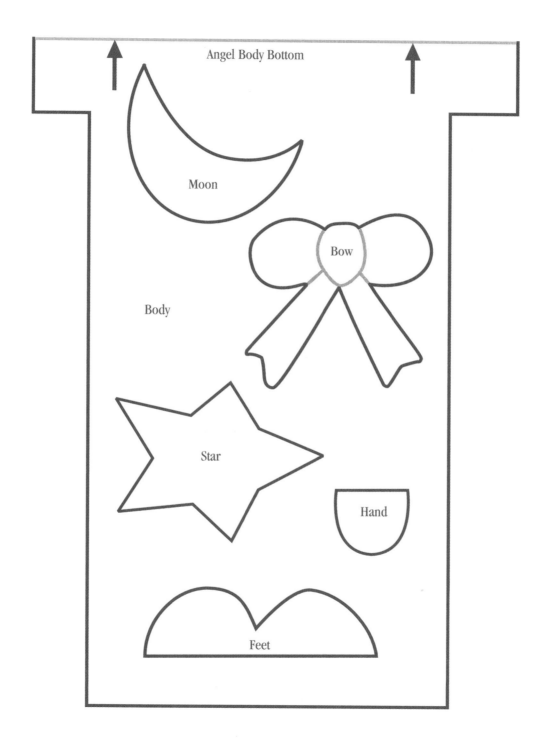

Angel Body Bottom

Moon

Body

Bow

Star

Hand

Feet

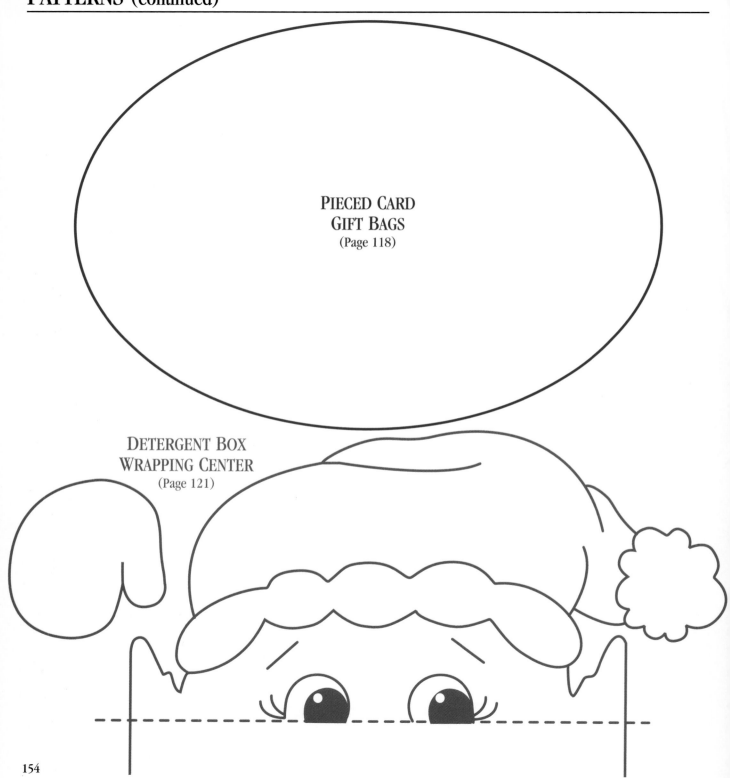

PIECED CARD
GIFT BAGS
(Page 118)

DETERGENT BOX
WRAPPING CENTER
(Page 121)

CROSS STITCH CANISTERS
(Page 127)

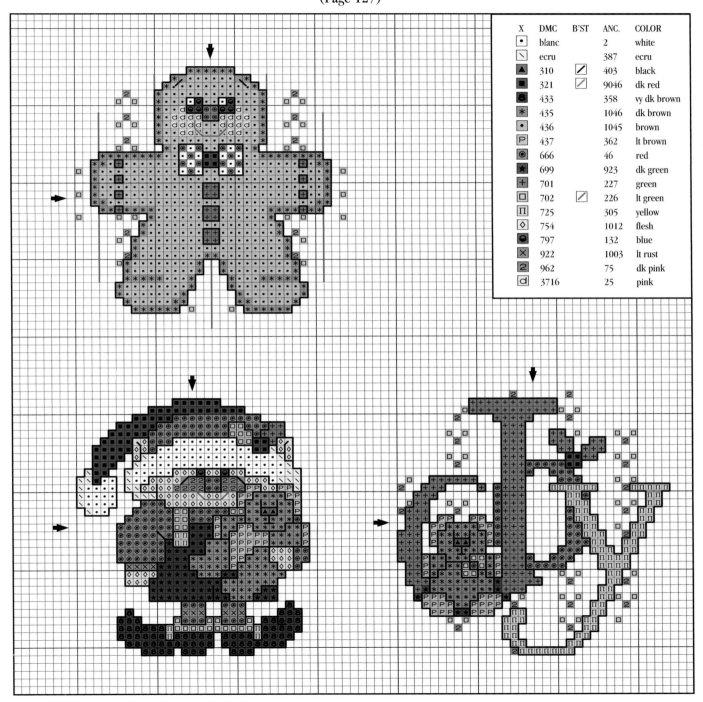

X	DMC	B'ST	ANC.	COLOR
•	blanc		2	white
◣	ecru		387	ecru
▲	310	╱	403	black
■	321	╱	9046	dk red
❂	433		358	vy dk brown
✳	435		1046	dk brown
•	436		1045	brown
P	437		362	lt brown
◉	666		46	red
★	699		923	dk green
+	701		227	green
□	702	╱	226	lt green
Π	725		305	yellow
◇	754		1012	flesh
◕	797		132	blue
✕	922		1003	lt rust
2	962		75	dk pink
d	3716		25	pink

General Instructions

Adhesives

When using any adhesive, carefully follow the manufacturer's instructions.

White craft glue: Recommended for paper. Dry flat.

Tacky craft glue: Recommended for paper, fabric, floral, or wood. Dry flat or secure items with clothespins or straight pins until glue is dry.

Craft glue stick: Recommended for paper or for gluing small, lightweight items to paper or another surface. Dry flat.

Fabric glue: Recommended for fabric or paper. Dry flat or secure items with clothespins or straight pins until glue is dry.

Decoupage glue: Recommended for decoupaging fabric or paper to a surface such as wood or glass. Use purchased decoupage glue or mix one part craft glue with one part water.

Hot or low-temperature glue gun: Recommended for floral, paper, fabric, or wood. Hold in place until set.

Rubber cement: Recommended for paper and cardboard. May discolor photos; may discolor paper with age. Dry flat (dries very quickly).

Spray adhesive: Recommended for paper or fabric. Can be repositionable or permanent. Dry flat.

Coffee Dyeing

1. Dissolve two tablespoons instant coffee in two cups hot water; allow to cool.
2. Soak fabric pieces in coffee several minutes. Remove from coffee; roll fabric between two towels to remove excess moisture. Allow to dry and press.

Making Patterns

For a more durable pattern, use a permanent pen to trace pattern onto stencil plastic.

WHOLE PATTERN
Place tracing paper over pattern and trace pattern; cut out.

SECTIONED PATTERN
Indicated by grey line on pattern.

1. Trace one pattern section.
2. Matching grey lines and arrows, trace remaining section to complete pattern; cut out.

Decoupage

1. Cut desired motifs from fabric or paper.
2. Apply decoupage glue to wrong sides of motifs.
3. Arrange motifs on project as desired, overlapping as necessary. Smooth in place and allow to dry.
4. Allowing to dry after each application, spray project with two to three coats of varnish.

Painting Techniques

TRANSFERRING A PATTERN
Trace pattern onto tracing paper. Place transfer paper coated side down between project and traced pattern. Use removable tape to secure pattern to project. Use a pencil to transfer outlines of design to project (press lightly to avoid smudges and heavy lines that are difficult to cover). If necessary, use a soft eraser to remove any smudges.

PAINTING BASE COATS
A disposable foam plate makes a good palette.

Use a medium round brush for large areas and a small round brush for small areas. Do not overload brush. Allowing to dry between coats, apply several thin coats of paint to project.

TRANSFERRING DETAILS
To transfer detail lines to design, reposition pattern and transfer paper over painted base coats and use a pencil to lightly transfer detail lines onto project.

ADDING DETAILS
Use a permanent pen to draw over detail lines.

DIMENSIONAL PAINT
Before painting on project, practice painting on scrap fabric or paper.

1. To keep paint flowing smoothly, turn bottle upside down and allow paint to fill tip of bottle before each use.
2. Clean tip often with a paper towel.
3. If tip becomes clogged, insert a straight pin into tip opening.
4. When painting lines or painting over appliqués, keep bottle tip in contact with surface of project, applying a line of paint centered over drawn line or raw edge of appliqué.
5. To correct a mistake, use a paring knife to gently scrape excess paint from project before it dries. Carefully remove stain with non-acetone nail polish remover. A mistake may also be camouflaged by incorporating the mistake into the design.
6. Lay project flat for 24 hours to ensure that paint has set.

SPONGE PAINTING

1. Dampen sponge with water.
2. Dip dampened sponge into paint; blot on paper towel to remove excess paint.
3. Use a light stamping motion to paint project.

MAKING APPLIQUÉS

To prevent darker fabrics from showing through, white or light-colored fabrics may need to be lined with fusible interfacing before applying paper-backed fusible web.

Follow all steps for each appliqué. When tracing patterns for more than one appliqué, leave at least 1" between shapes on web.

To make a reverse appliqué piece, trace pattern onto tracing paper; turn traced pattern over and continue to follow all steps using reversed pattern.

When an appliqué pattern contains shaded areas, trace along entire outer line for appliqué indicated in project instructions. Trace outer lines of shaded areas separately for additional appliqués indicated in project instructions.

Appliqués can be temporarily held in place by touching appliqués with tip of iron. If appliqués are not in desired position, lift and reposition.

1. Use a pencil to trace pattern onto paper side of web as many times as indicated in project instructions for a single fabric. Repeat for additional patterns and fabrics.
2. Follow manufacturer's instructions to fuse traced patterns to wrong side of fabrics. Do not remove paper backing.
3. Cut out appliqué pieces along traced lines. Remove paper backing.
4. Overlapping as necessary, arrange appliqués web side down on project.
5. Fuse appliqués in place.

MACHINE APPLIQUÉ

Unless otherwise indicated in project instructions, set sewing machine for a medium-width zigzag stitch with a short stitch length. When using nylon or metallic thread, use regular thread in bobbin.

1. Pin or baste a piece of stabilizer slightly larger than design to wrong side of background fabric under design.
2. Beginning on straight edge of appliqué if possible, position project under presser foot so that most of stitching will be on appliqué piece. Hold upper thread toward you and sew two or three stitches over thread to prevent raveling. Stitch over all exposed raw edges of appliqué and along detail lines as indicated in project instructions.
3. When stitching is complete, remove stabilizer. Pull loose threads to wrong side of fabric; knot and trim ends.

MAKING A BOW

Loop sizes given in project instructions refer to the length of ribbon used to make one loop of bow.

1. For first streamer, measure desired length of streamer from one end of ribbon; twist ribbon between fingers (Fig. 1).

Fig. 1

2. Keeping right side of ribbon facing out, fold ribbon to front to form desired-size loop; gather ribbon between fingers

(Fig. 2). Fold ribbon to back to form another loop; gather ribbon between fingers (Fig. 3).

Fig. 2

Fig. 3

3. If a center loop is desired, form half the desired number of loops, then loosely wrap ribbon around thumb and gather ribbon between fingers (Fig. 4). Continue to form loops, varying size of loops as desired, until bow is desired size.

Fig. 4

4. For remaining streamer, trim ribbon to desired length.
5. To secure bow, hold gathered loops tightly. Fold a length of floral wire around gathers of loops. Hold wire ends behind bow, gathering all loops forward; twist bow to tighten wire. Arrange loops and trim ribbon ends as desired.

WORKING WITH WAX

MELTING WAX

Caution: Do not melt wax over an open flame or in a pan placed directly on burner.

1. Cover work area with newspaper.
2. Heat 1" of water in a saucepan to boiling. Add water as necessary.

3. Place wax in a large can. If pouring wax, pinch top rim of can to form a spout. If dipping candles, use a can 2" taller than height of candle to be dipped.

4. To melt wax, place can in boiling water, reduce heat to simmer. If desired, melt pieces of crayon in wax for color. Use a craft stick to stir, if necessary.

SETTING WICKS

1. Cut a length of wax-coated wick 1" longer than depth of candle container.

2. Using an oven mitt, carefully pour wax into container.

3. Allow wax to harden slightly and insert wick at center of candle. Allow wax to harden completely.

EMBROIDERY STITCHES

BLANKET STITCH

Bring needle up at 1; keeping thread below point of needle, go down at 2 and come up at 3 (Fig. 1a). Continue working as shown in Fig. 1b.

Fig. 1a   Fig. 1b

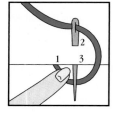
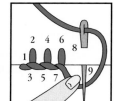

CHAIN STITCH

Bring needle up at 1 and down at 2, leaving a loop on top of fabric. Bring needle back up at 3 (Fig. 2a). Go back down at 4 and up at 5 (Fig. 2b) to make another loop. End chain by bringing needle up through last loop and back down just outside of loop.

Fig. 2a   Fig. 2b

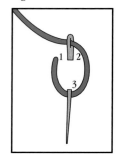
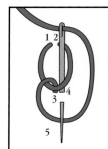

COUCHING STITCH

Thread first needle with desired number of threads or cord to be couched and bring up through fabric; hold threads or cord along desired line. Using a second needle, bring couching thread up at 1 and down at 2 to secure laid threads or cord (Fig. 3). Repeat to secure threads or cord along desired line.

Fig. 3

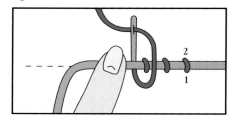

CROSS STITCH

Bring needle up at 1 and go down at 2. Come up at 3 and go down at 4 (Fig. 4).

Fig. 4

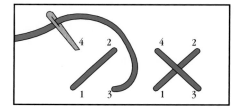

FEATHER STITCH

Bring needle up at 1 and down at 2, forming a "U" shape. Bring needle up at 3 inside stitch formed and then down at 4, forming another "U" (Fig. 5). End Feather Stitches by bringing needle up through last loop and straight down outside of loop.

Fig. 5

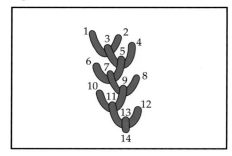

FLY STITCH

Bring needle up at 1 and down at 2, forming a "U" shape. Bring needle up inside "U" and straight down outside of "U" (Fig. 6).

Fig. 6

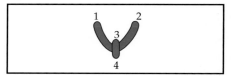

FRENCH KNOT

Bring needle up at 1. Wrap floss once around needle and insert needle at 2, holding floss with non-stitching fingers (Fig. 7). Tighten knot as close to fabric as possible while pulling needle back through fabric. For larger knot, use more strands of floss; wrap only once.

Fig. 7

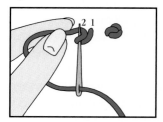

LAZY DAISY STITCH

Bring needle up at 1 and make a counterclockwise loop with thread. Go down at 2 and come up at 3, keeping the thread below point of needle (Fig. 8a). Secure loop by bringing thread over loop and going down at 4 (Fig. 8b).

Fig. 8a   Fig. 8b

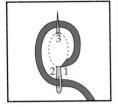

RUNNING STITCH

Make a series of straight stitches with stitch length equal to the space between stitches (Fig. 9).

Fig. 9

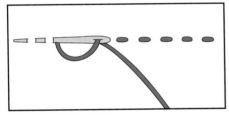

SATIN STITCH

Bring needle up at odd numbers and go down at even numbers with the stitches touching but not overlapping (Fig. 10).

Fig. 10

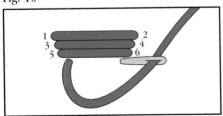

STRAIGHT STITCH

Bring needle up at 1 and go down at 2 (Fig. 11). Length of stitches may be varied as desired.

Fig. 11

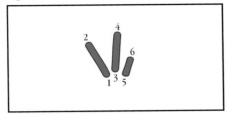

CROSS STITCH

PREPARING FABRIC

Use a wide zigzag stitch to sew around raw edges of Aida.

CROSS STITCH(X)

Work one Cross Stitch to correspond to each colored square in chart. For horizontal rows, work stitches in two journeys (Fig. 1). For vertical rows, complete each stitch as shown (Fig. 2).

Fig. 1

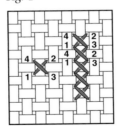

Fig. 2

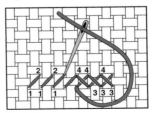

BACKSTITCH (B'ST)

For outline detail, Backstitch (shown on chart and color key by black or colored straight lines) should be worked after all Cross Stitch has been completed (Fig. 1).

Fig. 1

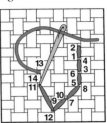

SEWING SHAPES

1. Center pattern on wrong side of one fabric piece and use fabric marking pen to draw around pattern. Do **not** cut out shape.
2. Place fabric pieces right sides together. Leaving an opening for turning, carefully sew pieces together **directly on drawn line** to join fabric pieces.
3. Leaving a $^1/_4$" seam allowance, cut out shape. Clip seam allowance at curves and corners. Turn shape right side out.

CREDITS

We want to extend a warm *thank you* to the generous people who allowed us to photograph our projects in their homes: Joan Adams, Shirley Held, Gwen Holton, and Duncan and Nancy Porter.

To Wisconsin Technicolor, Inc., of Pewaukee, Wisconsin, we say thank you for the superb color reproduction and excellent pre-press preparation.

We especially want to thank photographers David Hale, Jr., Mark Mathews, Larry Pennington, Karen Shirey, and Ken West of Peerless Photography, and Jerry R. Davis of Jerry Davis Photography, all of Little Rock, Arkansas, for their time, patience, and excellent work.

We would also like to recognize the River City Coffee, Tea, and Candy Company of Little Rock, Arkansas, for providing the divinity photographed with the *Soda Bottle Snowman*, page 46.

To the talented people who helped in the creation of the following projects in this book, we extend a special word of thanks:
- *Food Container Santa Ornaments*, page 77: Anne Fetzer
- *Cross Stitch Canisters*, page 127: Terrie Lee Steinmeyer

Thanks also go to the people who assisted in making and testing the projects in this book: Wanda J. Linsley, Patricia O'Neil, and Cynthia Sanders.